Functioning in Life as Gifts Given to the Body of Christ

WITNESS LEE

Living Stream Ministry
Anaheim, California

First Edition, August 2002.

ISBN 0-7363-1922-0

Published by

Living Stream Ministry
2431 W. La Palma Ave., Anaheim, CA 92801 U.S.A.
P. O. Box 2121, Anaheim, CA 92814 U.S.A.

Printed in the United States of America

02 03 04 05 06 07 08 / 10 9 8 7 6 5 4 3 2 1

CONTENTS

PREFACE

This book is composed of messages given by Brother Witness Lee in Los Angeles, California in the Summer Training of 1965. These messages were not reviewed by the speaker. The subject of the Summer Training was the inner life and the church life. The messages in this book were given concurrently with other messages on life and the church, including *Christ as the Content of the Church and the Church as the Expression of Christ* and *Dealing with Our Inward Parts for the Growth of Life.*

CHAPTER ONE

FUNCTIONING IN LIFE BY USING OUR TALENT

Scripture Reading: Matt. 25:14-30

With life there is always growth. Every kind of life grows. If something does not grow, it does not have life. Moreover, the growth of life is always for function. Every kind of life—whether animal life or vegetable life—grows for function. When a tree grows to a certain extent, it bears fruit. This bearing of fruit is the function of life. Animals also have their functions when they grow. Even when a small baby begins to grow, he has the function of life, and the more growth he has, the more function he has. Growth is for function.

THE NEED FOR ALL THE MEMBERS
OF THE BODY TO FUNCTION

The Bible tells us clearly that the church is the Body of Christ with many members, and all the members must function (Rom. 12:4-5). However, we must realize that function depends on the growth of life. If there is no life and no growth of life, there is no function. Function comes from growth, and growth is something of life. This is why Christianity has to have the system of clergy. Any kind of social body in the human community needs to hire someone to do certain duties. They also have to organize and form a board or committee from among its members, and they need to elect a leader, a secretary, and a treasurer. It is the same in principle in the so-called Christian churches. Because too many are dead in their spirit, they form an organization. There is no life and no function of life.

For many years my family was in such a place. However, I came out from that background, and so have many of you.

Still, we do not know how much we have been influenced by that background. Not only so, but the Christianity that surrounds us still unconsciously influences us. We do not have the sense that if we do not practice the function of life as members of the Body, there is something seriously wrong. If we do not function in the Body, we need to take this seriously. There is no need for me to preach to you, but I would ask you to be aware that if you are a brother or a sister, a member in the Body, but do not function, that is seriously wrong.

OUR FUNCTION DEPENDING ON THE GROWTH IN LIFE

We have to function, but function depends on growth. Why do many Christians today not function? It is because many Christians today do not grow. In the so-called churches today, it is hard to receive real nourishment, and there is no rich nourishment. Yes, there are some persons who have truly been saved and have life, but they do not have the adequate food. Today's Christianity is mostly a religion of teaching. The church, however, has to generate people and save people. This is why in the seven parables in Matthew 13 the Lord came not to teach people but to sow Himself as a seed into us. He came not to teach our mind but to sow Himself as the seed of life to grow in our heart. This is not to teach but to generate.

The Lord put Himself as the life-seed into us in order that we may grow, not into a great tree but as small wheat (v. 3). The purpose of wheat is to feed people. When wheat grows, it produces grains which can be used as food. The enemy's subtlety is first to snatch away the life-seed (vv. 4, 19). Second, he causes the heart to be hardened and stony so that the seed cannot grow, and third, he chokes the growth of the seed (vv. 5-7, 20-22). Eventually, though, the church must be like a little herb, like mustard. Mustard is good only for feeding people. The enemy, however, makes it into a great tree bearing no food (vv. 31-32). This is the situation of today's Christianity. It has become a big tree without food but with many places of lodging for "the birds of heaven," many evil persons and things. The church must be a little herb good for people to eat, but the enemy has changed the feeding nature of the church. It has become a "great tree" and has lost its function.

Today the Lord is going to recover the whole earth, but we are not here trying to be a big tree. Do not have that kind of thought. We must be delivered from degraded Christianity. The church on this earth is not for anything else but to grow as wheat to produce grains, or a little mustard herb, to feed people. A little herb can do nothing. It is good only for people to eat. In the church there is nothing but a wheat field, growing to produce not Ph.D.'s and professors but little grains to feed people. This is of basic importance. I hope that we all can see this.

I thank the Lord that right away after I was saved, He opened my eyes to see all these things, and He delivered me from the big tree. We have to realize that the Lord's recovery is the recovery of life. The Lord imparted Himself to us, and He feeds us day by day; as a result, we grow, and we function. We have received life; now we have to feed and feast on the Lord. Then we will grow, and we will function. Function comes from the growth of life.

THE MEMBERS BEING GIFTS,
WHOSE FUNCTION IS A MATTER OF LIFE

Now we may consider some passages in the New Testament concerning the function of life. Ephesians 4:7 to 16 shows us a principle related to our functioning. There is a difference between gifts and function. Many Christians do not differentiate these. With our two ears there is the function of hearing. However, the two ears themselves are a gift to the body. If there were no ears in the body, we could not hear. We would be short of a gift. We praise the Creator that He gave two ears to the body as a gift. Now this gift of two ears has the function of hearing, and this hearing function depends on life and the growth of life. The two ears of a baby have life, but with those ears there is the shortage of growth. The principle is that all the functions of the different parts of the body require a certain amount of growth. When the members come up to a certain extent of growth, they have the proper function. The member is a gift, but the function of the member is not a matter of gift. The function depends on the growth of life.

The gifts mentioned in Ephesians 4 are persons as the members, the big members—apostles, prophets, evangelists, and shepherds and teachers—and the smaller members (vv. 7-8, 11, 16). We might not be an apostle, prophet, evangelist, shepherd, or teacher, but we truly are members. Every member is a gift to the Body. If the Lord had not given me a stomach, how could I take in food? Even the tongue is a real gift from the Lord, the Divine Giver. How many times have we thanked the Lord that He gave us a tongue? We enjoy all the goodness from many different kinds of gifts, but we may never be grateful to the Lord, the Giver. However, if we were to lose one of our members, we would realize that is was a real gift.

Praise Him, all the members are gifts, and with every member as a gift there is a certain kind of function. The ears are a gift, the nose is a gift, and the two lips are a gift, but their functions are different. The function of the ears is to listen, the functions of the nose are to breathe and to smell, and the functions of the two lips are not to gossip but to praise the Lord and to take in nourishment.

The gifts in life in Romans 12:4 through 8 are different from the gifts mentioned in Ephesians 4:8, which refer to the gifted persons given by Christ in His ascension to His Body for its building up. The gifts in life in Romans 12 are also different from the miraculous gifts mentioned in 1 Corinthians 12 and 14. The gifts in life are developed by the growth in life and by the transformation in life (Rom. 12:2), out of the inward initial gifts mentioned in 1 Corinthians 1:7.

THE PARABLE OF THE TALENTS

Matthew 25:14 through 30 is the parable of the talents. Before this, however, there is the parable of the ten virgins (vv. 1-13). The parable of the virgins is a matter of life. Then after this life matter, there is the parable of the talents, which is a matter of function. Whereas virgins are for a pure life, talents are for service, for function. Here again we have the principle that function comes from life. In life we must be virgins, and in function we must use our talent. We need to see the basic principle for function in this portion of the Word.

Matthew 25:14 and 15 say, "For the kingdom of the heavens is just like a man about to go abroad, who called his own slaves and delivered to them his possessions. To one he gave five talents, and to another two, and to another one, to each according to his own ability. And he went abroad." The Lord mentioned five talents, two talents, and one talent. Since the Lord speaks this purposefully, there must be a meaning to it. Five is also mentioned in the previous parable. The ten virgins are divided into two groups of five each. This is very meaningful. According to the whole Bible, the number five signifies responsibility. Five is composed of four plus one. Consider our hands. The hand works, that is, it bears responsibility, by being four plus one. Four signifies the creature in creation, and one signifies the Creator. Four plus one is the creature plus the Creator to bear responsibility. We are the creatures, and the Creator has been added to us. Now we as the four plus one have to bear responsibility. The Lord numbers the talents from five because five signifies responsibility. Originally we were four, but since we received Christ into us, we are no longer four; we have become five.

Be careful when you read the Word, and learn the proper way to study it. On the one hand, we forget about mere teachings, but on the other hand, we need to have the right teachings. The Word of God is unique. No human mind can understand it in a mere human way. Rather, we must have revelation. Then the Word will be open to us. God is the God of Abraham, the God of Isaac, and the God of Jacob (22:32). Can we understand that in this title of God there is the indication of resurrection? This is the way the Lord expounded the Word. In 25:15 the Lord starts with the number five. Then He skipped over four because we can never be four again. Likewise, we can never be three since three signifies the Triune God. We were four, but now we are no longer four but five.

Two signifies testimony, or witness. All the functions of life are a testimony, a witnessing. A man has two shoulders, two arms, two hands, two ears, and two eyes. Everything is in twos. This is for balance, testimony, witness, and function. Many functions are in two. The listening is of two ears, the seeing is of two eyes, the smelling is of two nostrils, and the speaking is of two lips.

Why then did the Lord mention one? A person is one, and his body as a whole is also one. One signifies a complete unit. Regardless of how little we have received from the Lord, it is a complete unit. We have received "one." Someone may say, "I am too little a member." Yes, you may be the least, even less than the least, but you still must realize that you are a complete unit; you are one. This is very meaningful.

In verses 16 through 18 there are two key words. The Lord used one word for both the five-talented member and the two-talented member, and He used another word for the one-talented member. The key word for the five- and the two-talented members is *traded*. The five-talented one went to trade, and the two-talented one also went to trade. However, the word for the one-talented member is *dug*. The one-talented one dug in the earth and hid his lord's money.

The one with five talents made five more, and the one with two talents made two more. Why did they not make four, six, or seven more? We can never gain more than what the Lord gives us. In other words, we can never work out more than what we have received of the Lord. Whatever we work out must be the same as what we received from the Lord.

The principle related to function in this passage of the Word is that because we have been saved, we have received something, perhaps not five talents but two, or perhaps not two talents but one. If you say that you have not received even one, then you must not be saved. If we are saved, we have received at least one talent. Now we must go to trade, to use what we have received. This will produce something more. Five will produce five, and we will have ten. Two will produce two, and we will have four. At least one will produce one, and we will have double. The principle here is simply to function.

However, the one who received one talent did not function. Verse 18 says that he dug in the earth. Do you like to trade, or do you like to dig? It is easy to trade, but to dig is rather hard. Many brothers and sisters who do not function do a hard job day by day. They do the digging, not the trading. Those who do the digging are very busy not in the heavens but in the earth in order to hide their talent. The reason many Christians do not function is that they hide what they have. In their school they may never tell people what they have received of the Lord, and in the church meetings they also hide what they received of the Lord. The principle here is that we need to use the function that we have received. It should be normal for us to use it, not to hide it. We must encourage all the brothers, even the younger ones and the new converts, to use what they have received of the Lord and not to hide it.

The one who had the one talent said, "Master, I knew about you, that you are a hard man, reaping where you did not sow, and gathering where you did not winnow" (v. 24). Is this statement right or wrong? On the one hand, the Lord admitted to this, saying, "Evil and slothful slave, you knew that I reap where I did not sow and gather where I did not winnow" (v. 26). In another sense, though, it was not right for the evil slave to say that, because the Lord had sown one talent for him. The Lord did sow, and now He wants to reap something more. However, the Lord did not argue with the slave. He simply took his word to condemn him. Do not try to argue with the Lord. The more you argue, the more you will be condemned by your own word.

Verse 27 says, "Therefore you should have deposited my money with the money changers; and when I came, I would have recovered what is mine with interest." The Lord's money is His seed which He has sown. The slave should have deposited His seed, His money, with the money changers to make some interest. Here the Lord already had sown, and now He comes to reap. He had winnowed, and now He comes to gather. The slave should not have said that the Lord had not sown. He had sown one seed, one talent, into him. The slothful servant put the responsibility upon the Lord, saying, "You did not sow. You did not winnow. How can you reap and gather?" The Lord, however, returned the responsibility to his shoulder. The Lord did sow; He did give the slave one talent, so where is it now? The slave should have used the talent.

THE NEED FOR EVEN THE NEW ONES
AND YOUNG ONES TO FUNCTION

The principle in this passage is that we simply have to function. Simply learn to function. Many in Christianity have the thought that because some people cannot do anything, others should do everything for them. In some churches among us, the responsible brothers also have this wrong concept, saying, "These brothers and sisters do not know how to do something, so we will not let them do it. Let us do it instead." This is the wrong principle. Mothers do not say, "Do not ask my child to walk, because he does not know how." Rather, they know that the more their children walk, the more they are able to walk. Mothers simply encourage their child to walk, and they help a little by supporting him. Even if the child does not know how to walk, the mother at least encourages him to crawl, and eventually by crawling he learns to walk.

In the local meetings the responsible ones must encourage the brothers to function. Let them crawl; then they will learn to walk. Let them do something in the wrong way. Do not be afraid that your children will do something wrong; they need to do something wrongly, because they learn more in this way. We all learn by making mistakes. Help the new converts to function.

Many of the sisters who meet with us have been educated to be clever. Previously, more sisters prayed in the meeting, but now many are clever not to take any action. Then no one will know whether they are right or wrong. It is true that no one will know, but the sisters can never learn to function in this way. They have to pray; they have to function. Then they will learn. If you do not know how to walk, then simply crawl. You will learn how to walk by crawling. I do not like to have a Lord's table meeting with spiritual giants, in which everyone prays wonderfully, even better than the apostle Paul might have. That is not a sign of a healthy church. In the meeting for the Lord's table we need some experienced ones to pray, and we still need some spiritual babes to say something that a babe would say. This is beautiful and wonderful. The situation in a family should not be uniform. In a family there are the grandfather, grandmother, father, mother, older children, younger children, and even babies. There are many different voices; that is like music.

If there are only experienced ones, grandfathers and grandmothers, that is too old. Sometimes in a Lord's table meeting when all the experienced ones pray, there is the sense that the situation is too old. Encourage the brothers and sisters to function. Mothers know that for children to be naughty is one thing, but for them to do things in the wrong way is another thing; that is not naughty. For the younger ones and new converts to function in the church in a wrong way is not naughty. Rather, it is normal. Let them do something in the wrong way so that they may learn. Never consider that since they cannot do something or they do not know how to do it, we should not let them do it. This is the wrong idea. Let them do it. Let them try, and let them learn.

We all have to function. The principle for functioning is simply to function, to trade and not to dig in the earth. It is not to hide our talent but to use it. Then we will see the increase. The five will increase by another five, and eventually we get another one and another one. This is very meaningful. If you function, but I do not function when we meet together, eventually what I have will become yours. Whoever functions more gets more. Learn simply to function. Do not make any kind of argument or excuse. Do not say, "You are a hard man, reaping where you did not sow, and gathering where you did not winnow." We should not say this, and we should not take any excuse.

The right way, the normal way, is that everyone functions in the church, including the new converts, even the youngest among us. Although we do not have the clergy system in teaching, we may unconsciously practice it. On the Lord's Day certain brothers pray, and on the next Lord's Day the same ones pray. Out of one hundred twenty brothers meeting at the Lord's table, about forty always pray. The other eighty are the "laity." The whole year round, forty are traders, and eighty are diggers.

If a certain brother who always prays does not pray one day, the others will think it strange, because in their estimation he is one of the traders. Then if a certain sister prays, the saints will also be surprised. She is always a digger, but all of a sudden she rises up to be a trader. This is not normal. It should be that on one Lord's Day certain brothers pray, and on the next Lord's Day another group of brothers pray. Then throughout the year everyone prays. It will be hard to anticipate who will pray on a given day. In our present situation, however, we can tell which brother or sister will function, and we can even anticipate who will start the meeting and who will close the meeting. This is wrong. We have to do something to deal with this situation, to encourage all the brothers to pray.

This kind of situation is the context of 1 Corinthians 14. On the one hand, Paul says that the women should be silent, but on the other hand, he says that all can prophesy (vv. 24, 31). All the attendants in the meetings have not only the obligation but also the capacity to prophesy. God desires that each of the believers prophesy, that is, speak for and speak forth Him (v. 1b; cf. Num. 11:29).

CHAPTER TWO

THE GIFTS ACCORDING TO GRACE

Scripture Reading: Rom. 12:6a, 1-2, 11; Eph. 4:7-16

Apparently Romans 12 is easy to understand, but in actuality it is not easy to get into this portion of the Word. Again we may compare it to the title of God referred to by the Lord Jesus in Matthew 22:32: "The God of Abraham and the God of Isaac and the God of Jacob." It seems that it is easy to understand that God is the God of Abraham, the God of Isaac, and the God of Jacob. However, there is something in this title that requires a certain amount of spiritual insight. In Romans 12 it is the same in principle.

GIFTS DIFFERING ACCORDING TO GRACE

Verse 6a says, "And having gifts that differ according to the grace given to us." Here the gifts are according to grace. I am afraid that not many Christians know what *gifts...according to the grace* means. What is the grace mentioned here? What is the difference between gifts and grace? And what does it mean that gifts differ according to the grace? Grace may be compared to the blood supply in the members of our body. If a member has a bigger capacity for the blood supply, then it has a bigger gift. If it has a smaller capacity for the blood supply, the size of the gift in that member is smaller. In our little finger, the capacity for the blood supply is very small, so its gift, that is, its function, is also small in size.

In Romans 12 the gift is the function. Ephesians 4 tells us that the members are given to the Body as gifts, but Romans 12 tells us that the functions are given to the members as gifts respectively. In Ephesians 4 the gifts are to the Body while in Romans 12 the gifts are to the members. The latter gifts are the functions given to the separate members as gifts. The arm is given to a physical body as a gift. In addition, a gift is given to the arm as a function so that it can do something. This function is given to this member as a gift according to the measure of the capacity of how much blood supply the member has. If there is a bigger capacity for the blood supply to come in, then the gift is bigger. If there is a smaller capacity for the blood supply to come in, then the gift is smaller. Therefore, we can say that the gift, or the function, comes out of the capacity for the blood supply. This is the proper meaning of gifts differing according to the grace.

Grace is Christ as life to us, Christ within as the "blood supply," the life supply. As members, the kind of gift, or function, that we have depends on the quantity of Christ as life that we have. If we have more grace, that is, more Christ, then the function given to us will be bigger. If we have only a small amount of Christ, if our capacity to take Christ in is small and limited, we can have only a small function; the function that is given to us will be very limited. This is why Romans 12:6 tells us that the gifts differ according to the grace. The Lord gave the apostle Paul a very big function as a gift. If we had such a great capacity to contain Christ, we also would have a function like Paul's. The gift is given according to the capacity of grace, that is, of Christ as life.

BEING FREED FROM OCCUPATIONS
TO PRESENT OUR BODIES

How can we have the capacity to contain grace, Christ as life, within us? In Romans 12 there are three matters related to the three parts of our being. First, we have to offer our body (v. 1). This is to free our body. We should not let our body be occupied by things other than the Lord. Too often our body is occupied, not released. I agree that the young people have to study in college and the universities. I always encourage people to get a proper education. However, I am not happy to see the young brothers fully occupied by their studies. Sometimes they do not even come to the meetings because they say they are too busy. Their body is fully occupied by studies. I do not agree with this. To study is right, but it is not right to be fully occupied by studies.

It is the same with taking care of our home. To clean and keep our home in a proper way is right, but we should not be occupied in our body by housework. If our body is occupied by home affairs, then how can we function? I would suggest that if you do not have much time, then you should sacrifice a little of your studies and home affairs in order to set your body free from any kind of occupation, so that you may function and serve the Lord. In this country as well as in the Far East, some sisters and brothers keep their homes brilliant, but they do not have any time to contact the Lord. On the Lord's Day a sister may have time to come to the church meeting only to bring some money and drop it into the offering box. To her this means that she has done her duty. However, she may spend much time to keep her home with its decorations and bright floors.

To spend too much time keeping our home is a kind of luxury. We have to keep our home in a proper way, but only to that extent. Compare our situation with the lives of the Lord and the apostles. They did not spend time to prepare a brilliant home. We cannot bring our home into the New Jerusalem, so no doubt that is a waste. Eventually it will go into the "trash can," not into the New Jerusalem. If we spend too much time on something that will go to the trash can, it is better to spend it on something else. I do not agree that we should keep our home in a mess. We have to have a proper home, but only that much. Our body is too limited. We need to free our body for the Lord's service, for our function.

Why can we not function? It is because we are too occupied by our studies, our home, or our business. Some brothers are too occupied by their business. Last year they made five million dollars, this year they want to make eight million, and next year they want ten million. If they do this, they will not be able to serve. Learn to set your body free. Do not occupy it with so many things other than the Lord. This is the meaning of Romans 12:1, which tells us to present our bodies as a living sacrifice. We should not offer ourselves in an abstract way. We must have a concrete offering. The concrete offering is the offering of ourselves in our body. Everything must be done in our body. This is to set our body free from occupations and preoccupations.

BEING TRANSFORMED IN OUR SOUL

Second, we must be transformed in the soul by the renewing of our mind, the leading part of the soul (v. 2). Our body has to be offered, released, and set free from so many occupations, and our soul, our being, has to be transformed. We should not bring in old, natural concepts. The more we bring in natural concepts, the more we will be killed in function. In order to function in a proper, adequate way, we have to be transformed by the renewing of our mind. We need to have our mind renewed to have a new concept and new understanding.

BEING BURNING IN SPIRIT

Third, we have to be burning in our spirit (v. 11). Our body has to be offered, our soul has to be transformed, and our spirit has to be burning by contacting the Lord. We need to contact the Lord in the spirit continually. Then we will be on fire; we will be burning in spirit.

If we are short in any of the above matters related to the body, soul, and spirit, then we cannot function adequately. Someone may say that he has given up his business and is serving the Lord with his full time; thus, his body is released. That may be good, but what about transformation? What about the renewing of the mind? Someone may claim that he has studied in a seminary and graduated from a prestigious school. That is too old. That annuls his function. He has to be renewed in the mind. Someone else may say that he is a medical doctor or professor and that he knows many things. Do not say this; this will just kill you. Forget about those things. Our mind must be renewed. Someone else may say, "I am an experienced business man with a lot of knowledge of how to do things, manage, and organize." Forget about that too. That has to be put on the cross. A bank or a business corporation needs that, but the Body does not need it. You have to be renewed.

Someone else may say, "Praise the Lord, I have given up philosophy, a doctoral degree, my position as bank manager, and even the seminary." This is good. It means his mind is renewed. However, what about his spirit? Is his spirit on fire? This requires a continual contact with the Lord. Day by day and hour by hour we must be on fire in the spirit. If our body is offered, our soul is being transformed, and our spirit is also burning, then we will be able to function.

KEEPING THE PRINCIPLE TO CARE FOR OUR EXISTENCE WITHOUT BEING PREOCCUPIED

Our capacity for grace depends on these three things—we offer our body to the Lord, we are willing to be transformed, and we are burned by the Lord day by day. In this way we will have more capacity for grace, and Christ will come in and fill us. Then according to this capacity of grace, the Lord will give us a certain function as a gift, and we ourselves will become a gift given to the Body. We must first be in Romans 12, and then we can be in Ephesians 4. When our body is offered, our being, our soul, is transformed, and our spirit is on fire, we have the capacity for the Lord to come in as our grace. We will be filled with grace, and out of this grace and based upon this grace, a certain function will be given to us as a gift. Spontaneously we will receive a gift, and then as members we will be gifts to the Body. In this way the Body will be rich, and it will be built up.

Suppose that all the brothers and sisters are occupied. The young brothers and sisters are occupied by their studies and their degree: first their B.A., then their M.A., then one Ph.D., and then another. The mothers are occupied by their children, the housewives are occupied by their homes, and the brothers are occupied by their business. Can we have the Body in this way? In one place a brother told me, apparently with a good spirit, "Today is a day of science, so anything that we do, we have to do it scientifically. In any kind of business or operation, there is a scientific way to carry it out. In the church life we must apply this principle. We should not expect every brother or sister to minister and function. Some have to study, some have to take care of their children, some have to take care of their homes, and some have to take care of their business. They simply do not have the time to function in the church. Therefore, it is right to train someone to be an expert. Then the church can pay him to function." This thought is something of the natural concept. The church is not a social body. The church is the Body of Christ, and we all are members of this Body. Can a member of the Body say, "I have too many things to take care of, so I am willing to pay the shoulder to take care of my function"? If one member can say this, then all the members can say it also. Then what kind of body would that be? That would not be a body at all.

We all have to realize that we are here on this earth not for study, for our home, or for our business. We are priests on this earth to serve the Lord. We are living here for the service, for the testimony of the Lord, just as the priests did. Of course, we need something for our existence. We need food, clothing, housing, marriage, and children for our existence; there is no doubt about this. However, we should not sacrifice the service for our existence. Our existence is for the service. If we cannot release ourselves, how can we serve?

The proper principle is that we have to be balanced. If you are a student who must study very hard, if possible, you should reduce your studies a little in order to set your body free with respect to your time. You may have to take more time to finish your education in order to save some time for your body to be released. In addition, if you can live not in a luxurious way but in a proper way by making a certain amount of money each month, that is good enough. Do not work more to make more money. That is to sell yourself to the slavery of money. To have a proper, healthy, good life up to a certain standard is good enough. Do not raise your standard of living. If you raise your standard, you will sell yourself to the slavery of a high standard of living. This is the subtlety of the enemy. We should always keep our living simple without damaging our physical life. As long as we live in a healthy way, that is good enough. Then we can save our time and energy for the service, and we will have the capacity for grace. No doubt, we should not neglect our children. We have to raise our children and care for them, but we should not care too much. We should keep a balance. We are not here on this earth for our children. We are here for the service. Our housing, our food, our clothing, our marriage, our family, and our children are all for our existence, and our existence is for the service. Why can Christians today not function? It is because their bodies are occupied and preoccupied. A millionaire can give ten thousand dollars a year to the church to fund a building, but he may not be able to function. The Lord does not want these things. Ten thousand, one hundred thousand, and millions of dollars mean nothing to Him. The Lord wants us. According to Romans 12:1, He wants us to offer our body as a living sacrifice. What matters to the Lord is not money but the living person, our body. We have to release our body from so many occupations.

We look to the Lord's mercy. When we speak of the Lord's recovery, we include this matter. There must be a group of Christians in the United States who truly live for the Lord. We must live in a proper way, not in a poor way as beggars, and we may even live richly, but nothing occupies us (1 Tim. 6:6-10). We are existing here for the divine service. There is no doubt that we should encourage our young people to study and graduate from school with a proper education. We also must encourage our sisters to take care of their homes and to raise children in a proper way. However, we have to keep a balance and keep the principle. We are here not for our studies, not for the family, not for raising children, not to care for homes, and not for doing business. We are here for the service. In order that we may live, that we may exist, we need these things, but only up to a proper standard. Nothing should preoccupy us.

INCREASING OUR CAPACITY FOR GRACE IN ORDER TO RECEIVE A GREATER GIFT

To have the Lord's recovery is not merely to have the doctrine of the recovery. No, we must be in Romans 12, offering our body, being transformed in our being—our soul with the mind as the leading part—and being burned in our spirit all the time. It is based on these three items that we will have the capacity for grace. Grace will come in to fill us, and from this grace and according to this grace, certain functions will be given to us as gifts. We all will have a gift, that is, a function, and we will be equipped with this gift. Then we ourselves will become living gifts given to the Body. It is by these living gifts given to the Body that the Body will be built up. I do ask you to pray for this. I do not want merely to be a teacher, passing on a teaching to you. Rather, I want to burden you with this matter. Please bring this to the Lord in prayer.

We have to dress ourselves neatly and properly, but we, especially the sisters, should not be preoccupied with our dress. To many women dressing becomes an occupation. We should care for our dress and use our money and energy only to the extent of being proper and neat, and no more (1 Tim. 2:9-10). Dress is a real temptation to women. It is the same throughout the whole world. Sisters, if you love the Lord and if you mean business with the Lord, simply dress yourselves to a proper and neat extent. Never spend one cent more or one minute more for dressing. In terms of money, time, and energy you have to limit yourselves. Then you will be released. You will see how much grace you will receive and how much your capacity to receive Christ will be enlarged, and you will see a bigger, higher function given to you as a gift. You will be equipped by this gift, and you will become a living gift to the Body. Then the Body will be enriched by you. The whole Body will be built up. This is something different from today's Christianity. We are speaking here about the Lord's recovery.

We must keep the practical things among us. We should dress ourselves properly, care for our home properly, raise our children properly, and do our business properly. However, we must always keep a limit, do these things only up to a certain extent, and not be tempted by the enemy to go further. We must keep ourselves within a limit in order to set ourselves free from any kind of occupation or preoccupation. Then the body will be offered completely, and our soul will be transformed. We will have the time to contact the Lord, and we will always be on fire in our spirit. Then we will have the capacity for more grace to come in.

While Brother Watchman Nee was studying in college, he gave at least half of his time for the Lord's service and still excelled in his studies. We have to be balanced and limited. Then we will have more capacity for the Lord and His grace. Otherwise, we are merely speaking doctrines, listening and learning but without practice. All these things will be proved and tested by the Lord's coming and at His judgment seat (2 Cor. 5:10). We must not reckon that our business is something only for ourselves. We need to say, "Lord, I am not here for my business. I am here for Your service. I am doing a business not for myself but for Your service." I do believe that the Lord will recover a group of people who live on the earth in this way. They will come together to exalt Christ. They will experience Christ in a practical way, and all kinds of functions will come out.

GRACE GIVEN ACCORDING TO THE GIFT

Ephesians 4:7 seems to say something contrary to Romans 12. Romans 12 says that the gifts are according to grace, but this verse in Ephesians says, "But to each one of us grace was given according to the measure of the gift of Christ." Here grace is given according to the gift. The gifts mentioned in Romans are the functions given to the members, but the gifts mentioned in Ephesians 4 are the members given to the Body. Gifts as functions are according to the grace, but grace is given according to the persons as gifts. Because you are a certain member, you need a certain amount of grace. If you are a big member, you need a bigger quantity of the "blood supply." The blood supply is given according to our gift as a member.

This chapter also tells us that the bigger gifts are for perfecting the smaller ones (vv. 11-12). The bigger members are to perfect the smaller ones, not to replace them. In turn, the smaller members must learn to receive the perfecting of the bigger ones. Do not think that this is easy. It is easy to let others replace us, saying, "I do not want to do this. It is too troublesome. Let us hire a pastor to do it for us." On the other hand, though, if we do something, we do not want to receive any kind of perfecting from others. If we do it, we feel that we know how to do it, and we want to do it by ourselves. If someone tries to perfect us, we may say, "I quit. You do it. Otherwise, keep away, let me do it, and don't say anything." It is the same with the brothers, the sisters, and even the younger ones. In the home the children never like the parents to say something. They want to do things independently. In the church, however, we must do things by being perfected by the bigger members. We need to function, but we must do it by being perfected by others.

In Ephesians 4 we again see the need for growth. Verse 13 speaks of a full-grown man, and verse 15 says that we grow up into Him in all things, who is the Head, Christ. In this chapter we also see the coordination of the Body and that all the functions, regardless of what kind they are, must be for the building up of the Body (v. 16). Grace is given according to the gift, the bigger gifts are for the perfecting of the smaller ones, and the smaller gifts have to function under the perfecting of the bigger ones. Moreover, all the members must grow, function in coordination, and be for the building up of the Body. Then we will function properly. This is on the positive side. Then on the negative side, there are the winds of teaching that blow the members away from the Head and the Body (v. 14). This is not the wind of heresy, but the wind of correct doctrine used too much in the wrong way to blow and carry away. To no longer be little children tossed by waves and carried about by every wind of teaching, we need to grow up into Christ. This is to have Christ increase in us in all things until we attain to a full-grown man.

CHAPTER THREE

THE MEMBERS GIVEN AS GIFTS TO THE BODY

Scripture Reading: Psa. 68:18; Eph. 4:7-16

In the previous message we saw that grace is given according to the measure of the gift of Christ (Eph. 4:7). There is a very deep meaning in this. It is not easy to have this kind of concept, but if we have the heavenly, spiritual insight, we can see the real meaning here. Ephesians 4 quotes from Psalm 68:18, which says, "You have ascended on high; You have led captive those taken captive; / You have received gifts among men, / Even the rebellious ones also, / That Jehovah God may dwell among them." *You* here refers to Christ; this passage is concerning the ascension of Christ.

CHRIST RECEIVING GIFTS AMONG MEN

Darby's New Translation renders *You have received gifts among men* as, "Thou hast received gifts in Man," and his footnote says, "i.e. as man..., in connection with mankind." Christ ascended on high, He led captive those taken captive, and He received gifts in men and as men; that is, He received the rebellious ones as gifts. His purpose in doing this was that He may build up His dwelling place on this earth among the rebellious men. He did this for the building up of the church. The last phrase, *that Jehovah God may dwell among them,* is not quoted in Ephesians 4:7, but the context of Ephesians deals with God's dwelling place. By this we can truly see that the Bible was not written according to the human mind or concept. We could never conceive such a truth merely with the human concept. Rather, the Bible was written by the Holy Spirit (2 Pet. 1:21; 2 Tim. 3:16).

EVERY MEMBER HAVING A GIFT AND BEING A GIFT

The gifts mentioned in Ephesians 4 are the members, the gifted persons. The members of the Body are the gifts given to the Body. Every member of the Body is a gift, not only the apostles, prophets, evangelists, and shepherds and teachers (v. 11), but even the smallest member is a gift. Even our little finger is a gift. Many times I have been grateful to the Lord that I have a little finger. Whenever there is an itching in my ear, nothing can help me but my little finger. I am grateful to the Lord that we have a gift that is so small yet so practical. The little finger is a practical gift to the body; it truly helps. If you lose your little finger, you will see how awkward it is not to have it. When we have such a member, we may not sense its practicality, but if we were to lose it, we would sense the awkwardness of not having it. Every member of the body is a gift.

Not many Christians, including many Christian teachers, know what the difference is between the gifts mentioned in Romans 12 and the gifts mentioned in Ephesians 4. Even if some may know the difference, they do not have the utterance to speak it. The proper utterance is to say that whereas the gifts mentioned in Romans 12 are the functions given to the members, the gifts in Ephesians 4 are the members given to the Body. We may illustrate this difference with our ears and eyes. An ear without the hearing function is a poor, useless ear. However, the Lord is full of grace to give a function to the ear. The hearing function was given to this ear as a gift, so the ear itself becomes a gift to the body. Similarly, an eye specialist can give you an artificial eye, but that is an eye without the seeing function, without a gift. The seeing function is a gift to the eye as a member. Then because the eye has the gift of the seeing function, it can now be given to the body as a gift. The function is a gift to the member, and the member is a gift to the body.

THE GIFT BEING ACCORDING TO THE GRACE

The gift in Romans 12 is given according to the grace. This means that the function given to the members is based on the life in the members. If there were no blood supply to my eyes, they would lose their function. The eyes also need vitamin A. If I did not take any vitamin A for a period of time, my two eyes would lose their function. The function of the eyes is given according to the inner vitamin A. Grace is our "vitamin A." The gift given to the members of the Body is according to the grace, the inner life supply, the inner "vitamins." If the members have the inner vitamins, they will have a function, but without the inner vitamins, the inner grace, the life supply, their function will be lost. We need the inner life. All the functions mentioned in Romans 12 require the inner supply.

GRACE BEING GIVEN ACCORDING TO THE MEASURE OF THE GIFT

In Ephesians 4 the gifts are the members, and grace is given according to the size of the members, that is, according to the measure of the gift. Just as blood is supplied to a member of our body according to its measure, its size, grace is given to the members of the Body of Christ according to their measure as a gift. The inner supply is given according to the size of the members. If someone is a big member, he has a bigger capacity for more grace, but if he is a small member, his capacity to receive grace is smaller.

CHRIST PRODUCING THE GIFTS THROUGH HIS DEATH, RESURRECTION, ASCENSION, AND OUR REGENERATION

We are the members of the Body, but in the past we were not members. A member is not merely a person. There are millions of persons in Los Angeles, but only a small number of these persons are the members of the Body. The difference between a member of the Body of Christ and a person who is not a member is regeneration. A person who has never been regenerated is only a person, not a member of the Body of Christ. To be regenerated is to have the Triune God—the Father, the Son, and the Spirit—come into the tripartite man to become life in his spirit. Now this man has the divine life as a life in addition to his created human life (1 Pet. 1:3; John 3:6; Col. 3:4).

Producing the Gifts through His Death, Resurrection, and Ascension

However, the story of our regeneration is not this simple. The Triune God is the Father in the Son and the Son as the Spirit (John 14:10a; 1 Cor. 15:45b). One day this One was incarnated, became a man, and lived on this earth among men and as a man. Then He went into death and came out of death in resurrection. He ascended and was enthroned with authority and a kingdom. Do not think that this is merely my concept. This is according to Psalm 68:18: "You have ascended on high; You have led captive those taken captive." This implies that by His death and resurrection the Lord Jesus fully dealt with the enemy Satan. By His death and resurrection Christ has captured and disarmed Satan's capturing power. In a battle, the one who conquers disarms the one who is defeated. This captures away all the fighting power of the defeated one. The Lord Jesus Christ by His death and resurrection captured all the capturing power of the enemy, as Hebrews 2:14 says, "Through death He might destroy him who has the might of death, that is, the devil." The might of death is the capturing power of the enemy, which was captured away. In this sense, *led captive those taken captive* in Psalm 68:18 implies that the Lord, the ascended One, passed through death and resurrection and by death and resurrection captured the capturing power of Satan. This Psalm, therefore, speaks of the ascension of Christ and implies His crucifixion and resurrection.

Producing the Gifts through Regeneration

Now Christ has ascended to the heavens and is enthroned there as a man, and in man with man's nature, He received gifts. It is this wonderful One who comes into our spirit to produce the members. Therefore, *You have received gifts among men* implies a deep matter. As a man, representing man, in man, and with man, Christ received the gifts. The incarnated, crucified, resurrected, and ascended Christ with the divine nature and the human nature comes into us to regenerate us for the purpose of producing members.

The gifts are the members, the members are produced through regeneration, and regeneration implies all of the above matters. Before we were regenerated, that is, before we were saved, we were sinful, dead, and under the captivity of Satan. We had sin in the body, self in the soul, and death in the spirit, and we were under the darkness of Satan. We were captured as captives. We had nothing of God but many things of Satan. How could we get rid of all these negative things, on the one hand, and on the other hand, have the Triune God in us as our life? This could be accomplished only by the all-inclusive dose—all that the Triune God is, including His uplifted, transformed human nature and all His dealings through death and resurrection. By death and resurrection the Lord captured all the capturing power of Satan. This includes the Lord's dealing with sin, the self, death, and darkness. Everything of Satan has been dealt with by the death and resurrection of Christ. Now the effectiveness of His death and the power of His resurrection are all included in an all-inclusive dose. When this dose comes into us, it right away dissolves death, self, sin, and darkness, on the negative side, and it brings the Triune God into us, on the positive side. We cannot exhaust the revelation of all that this all-inclusive dose is. His purpose in coming into us was to produce members, and all the members are gifts. This is the way He received gifts among men.

After the Lord's ascension but before our regeneration, Christ still had not received us as gifts in a practical sense. We were still under darkness with sin, self, and death. However, when the Triune God came in to deal with our death, self, sin, and darkness and to impart Himself into us with His uplifted human nature, we were produced as gifts. Practically speaking, it was at this point that Christ received us as gifts. It will help us to understand this better if we consider that to receive gifts means to produce gifts. Christ passed through death and resurrection, and in doing so He captured the capturing power of Satan. This means that He solved all the negative problems by His death and resurrection. Then He ascended to receive, that is, to produce, the gifts. Yet how are the members of the Body of Christ produced, obtained, and gained as gifts in a practical sense? It is by this wonderful One coming into fallen persons to regenerate them.

After this He gave all the gifts whom He received, gained, obtained, and produced to the Body. Now all these gifts put together are the Body. The original speaking in Psalm 68:18 says that He received gifts, but the quotation in Ephesians 4:8 says that He gave gifts. First He received the gifts, and then He gave what He received. Eventually, His receiving was His giving. When He produced the members, right away the members became gifts to the Body.

The Father is the source, and all the gifts came from this source. These gifts were received by Christ the Son and were transmitted by the Spirit to the Body. Therefore, to say that Christ produced the gifts means both that He received them and that He gave them. When the gifts were produced, they were received, and when they were received, they were given. The Body of Christ is composed with all the members, all the members are gifts, and the gifts were produced by the work of the Triune God, including our regeneration. This is not the human concept. This is the revelation in the Word of God.

The Head of the Body is the Triune God with His humanity, human living, death, resurrection, ascension, enthronement, and authority. The members of the Body are the big members and the small members. All the members have different measures, different sizes, and grace is given to each one of the members according to its measure as a gift. This grace is Christ as the inner life supply, the "blood supply," the inner "vitamins," and it is given according to the measure of the gift, that is, according to the size of the member. If someone is a big member like Paul, a large life supply is ministered to him, but if he is a small member, he receives a smaller life supply.

PRINCIPLES FOR THE MEMBERS
AS GIFTS TO THE BODY

Concerning the members as gifts to the Body, there are at least three principles. First, the gifts mentioned in Ephesians 4 are the members, and the members are the regenerated, remade man, not the natural man. Therefore, anything natural has to be rejected. In order to minister, to function, in the church, we first must reject the natural man. Whatever we are naturally, we have to reject. The more we reject the natural man, the more useful we will be.

Second, we must always realize the death, resurrection, and ascension of Christ. We have been crucified, buried, and resurrected, and we have ascended with Him. Now we are in the heavens. Again, this is not merely my concept. Before chapter four of Ephesians there is chapter two, which tells us that we have been raised up together with Christ and seated together with Him in the heavenlies (v. 6). Negatively, we have to deny the soul, the natural man, and positively, we have to realize that we are now in the heavenlies. All earthly and negative things are under our feet. This is the nature and position of the members of the Body. The nature of the members is the divine, resurrected, uplifted nature, and the position of the members is in the heavenlies.

Third, we have to constantly receive grace and let His life be our inner supply. If we do not receive grace, the inner supply of life, we become useless, withered members. When a member does not have the blood supply, it becomes withered and cannot function. We need the new circulation of the blood supply by fellowshipping with and contacting the Lord as the Head. Then we will be living and able to function.

If we see these matters, we will be very confirmed and strengthened to know the right way to function. We must realize that now we are members of the Body; we are not a natural man, a person living on this earth merely for this earth. Moreover, we are sitting in the heavenlies, and we continually contact the Lord as our life supply. We need a clearer apprehension of these spiritual matters and of all the revelations in the New Testament.

CHAPTER FOUR

PERFECTING THE MEMBERS
FOR THEIR FUNCTION

Scripture Reading: Eph. 4:13-16

In order to perfect others, the first thing we must do is minister life to them to help them to grow. Then we must give them the opportunity to serve, that is, to function. It is very easy for the bigger members to take all the opportunities. It is rather hard, on the other hand, for the younger ones, the smaller ones, to get the opportunity. Whether or not they get the opportunity to function depends on the attitude and way of the bigger members. In addition, we need to teach the members some techniques for functioning.

NOT REPLACING BUT PERFECTING
THE SMALLER MEMBERS

Humanly speaking it is too easy for a bigger member to replace others. Whenever a bigger member functions, there is the danger of replacing others, especially the smaller ones. This is because the bigger ones think that they can do something that the smaller ones cannot do. It is also easy for a member to do something by himself and more difficult to do something with others. Many times in my Christian life of service, some, especially the sisters, have told me, "If I do this, I will do it myself. Do not let anyone come to bother me." When some sisters cook, they say "Get out of the kitchen. Let me do the cooking. If you do it, do it yourself, but if I do it, I will do it by myself."

It is truly hard to bring someone in to help us and learn with us. To have an apprentice becomes a problem. However, consider the apostle Paul. He always had a younger, smaller one—such as Timothy or Titus—to help him and learn from him. We have to keep this principle. If we are a member that is bigger than others, we should never replace them. Rather, we must give others the opportunity to practice and to learn.

Even in the matter of attending the meeting, we need to help the younger ones. We may notice that a younger brother has not prayed in the meeting for more than two months. Perhaps by the Lord's sovereign arrangement he may live close by in the same neighborhood. In this case, we need to do something to help this younger brother by having some fellowship about the meetings. We may say, "Brother, don't you feel that we should pray in the meeting?" He may say that he does not know how to pray. We may answer, "Simply open to the Lord to express something from your spirit. Brother, may we pray together now? If you do not know how to pray, simply exercise your spirit to touch the Lord and utter something from within. When you contact the Lord, you must have the cleansing of the blood of Jesus. If you feel that you are wrong, then tell that to the Lord. If you feel that you have some failures, confess them to Him and apply His cleansing blood."

Before the Lord's table meeting on the next Lord's Day, we can invite the brother to dinner. Then we can take the opportunity to help him further. We can ask, "Brother, are you ready to offer a prayer in the Lord's table meeting?" If he says he does not know what to pray, we can explain how the church is are about to come together to remember the Lord, enjoy Him, and partake of Him. Then we may have a time to pray with him: "Lord, help us tonight that we may have something with which to express You." In this way we can minister something to the younger brother. How much we can teach and minister to such a one depends on how much we learn and experience. We all have to learn how to raise up the younger ones.

Before we come to the meeting, we can talk with the young brother and help him to know how to choose a hymn and do various things. After this, we come to the meeting and sit with him. At a certain point in the meeting, it may be time to announce a particular hymn. We can then ask the brother to announce it. This may be the first time that he calls a hymn. We should open the way for him. We can start something, but he should carry it out. After another half hour, we may feel that the brother should pray or praise in the meeting, and we can help him to do it.

After the meeting we can have a little fellowship with him. We can read that hymn again with him and explain why it needed to be called at that certain time, and we can explain why he needed to pray at a certain time. He will realize something and learn from this. Then he may ask, "Do you think I have prayed in the right way?" In doing this, he will open the way for us to give him some correction, instructions, or ministry. Within a short time of doing this, we will have a "graduate." Then this brother will know how to help others. If we know this principle, we can apply it to all the services, even in the small matters. This requires that we have a real love for the Lord and a real love and concern for the Body.

The way to bring all the members into function is not merely by teaching. Mothers do not mostly teach their children. Mainly they simply help them. Then the children learn. We have to give the young ones the opportunity to do something. The principle is that in whatever we do, we must never replace others. All year round we may always pray three or four times in every meeting. However, we need to learn how to bring others into this function, not to replace them but to perfect them.

When we perfect others, we have to minister life to them. As I illustrated above, we may share with a brother that he should open himself to the Lord, confess his failures, and contact the Lord. This is not merely a way but a ministry of life. Then to explain why a particular hymn should be announced or why someone should offer a prayer about the Lord's glory at a certain time may be considered a teaching of ways, or techniques. With everything and in whatever we do, we have to do it with someone to help us so that they may learn from us. In this way we will continually produce and reproduce. Then one brother produces many brothers, and those many brothers reproduce another number of brothers and sisters. We all need to learn this.

Spontaneously, there will be a certain kind of realization among us. The younger ones will submit to the older ones to be perfected, and the smaller ones will submit to the bigger ones. Merely to say that the younger and smaller ones have to submit does not work. We cannot make this claim. Rather, we must have the proper practice. Then spontaneously the younger ones and smaller ones will submit to others to be perfected. This depends not as much on the smaller ones as on the bigger ones. In everything, in every aspect of the service, we must apply the same principle.

THE TESTIMONY OF A PERFECTING MEMBER

When I was young, by the Lord's mercy I came in contact with Brother Watchman Nee, and under the Lord's sovereignty I was put under his hand. On the one hand, he did not merely teach me, but on the other hand, he taught me very much. Once in 1933 the church in Shanghai was to have a gospel preaching meeting. The responsible ones thought that Brother Nee would prepare to give the message. When they contacted him, however, he said, "Ask Brother Lee to do it." Then those responsible ones came to me and put me into the position of having to give a message for the gospel. When I asked where Brother Nee would be, they said, "He is probably busy. Perhaps he will be out of the city. Now you must do it." Of course, I did give the message. Eventually, though, I found out that behind the platform that I stood on, there was a small back door, and throughout my whole message Brother Nee was standing there listening to me. I can never forget that. It was the first time I received the light concerning John 16. Concerning the Spirit of reality, verse 8 says, "When He comes, He will convict the world concerning sin and concerning righteousness and concerning judgment." The Spirit convicts concerning three things. He convicts concerning sin because we are in Adam, concerning righteousness because we need to be transferred into Christ, and concerning judgment because if we are still in Adam and not willing to be transferred into Christ, we will be judged with Satan.

Two or three weeks later, as Brother Nee and I were sitting in his living room, he said, "Brother Lee, it was a real light that to be convicted of sin means that someone is in Adam, of righteousness that he needs to be in Christ, and of judgment that he follows Satan." I did not know from where he had heard this. Eventually I was told that he was at the back door listening to the entire message. It was at that time that he encouraged me, saying, "Brother, you have to go out to teach people according to your understanding of the Bible."

At about that time, around eight of us under thirty years old were all learners. We had no intention to do anything but to stay there day by day to learn. Brother Nee always gave the messages. One Lord's Day morning we all came to the breakfast happy that we were about to hear Brother Nee speak another message. Since we were learners, we just wanted to hear him. The meeting started at 10:00. That morning, a brother who helped with the cooking came to me at about 9:30 or 9:40 with a small slip of paper from Brother Nee. It said, "Please give the message this morning." After he delivered the note, the brother disappeared, so I did not know what to do. Before this time, however, I had had much contact with Brother Nee in which he had spontaneously given me help and instructions on the ministry of life, and through this I had received something. When that note came, therefore, I did have something to minister. As I was standing there to give a message, I was on the test. Brother Nee did not come to the meeting, but I knew that in the afternoon he would come to certain older ones to ask the full story about what I had ministered. Later, perhaps after two or three weeks, we were together in a car, and as he was driving, he spoke with me, referring to my message.

On another occasion when I was asked to give a message on the Lord's Day, I spoke in a strong and detailed way on how to abide in the Lord. I was very burdened, and I thought that I had given a good message. Again, Brother Nee was not there. After a certain number of days, he told one of the elder sisters who lived close to me, "Please say to Brother Lee that if we are in Christ, there is no need for us to learn how to be in Him." Later, when I went to sit with these elder sisters, one said, "Brother Lee, Brother Nee asked me to tell you one thing. If we are in Christ, there is no need for us to learn how to be in Christ." This truly opened my eyes. I am in the United States, so there is no need for me to learn how to be in the United States. In the same way, we do not need to learn how to abide in Christ but rather to realize that we are in Him already. These stories illustrate Brother Nee's way of perfecting the members.

We all must learn the lesson not to replace others but always to produce and perfect them. In addition, we must have the growth of life. Then we will know how to minister life to others. Raising up others has many problems, but those are the lessons we have to learn. We have to learn to perfect others in many ways, including how to help them to study the Word, to contact people, and to visit people. Then the whole church will be functioning.

THE ATTITUDE OF THE SMALLER MEMBERS

In the church the bigger members must learn to perfect others, and the smaller, younger members must learn to take the perfecting. This is not merely to submit but to receive perfecting. In the early days, by the Lord's true mercy I was a learner. I made a decision within myself simply to be a learner. Many times I was asked to suggest something, but I only answered, "I have no suggestion." I simply wanted to do whatever the perfecting members told me. If we receive perfecting from others, we will learn more.

If someone says, "Brother, would you please give a message?", the best thing to do is ask, "What message should I give?" If the perfecting one says, "You may minister something about the inner life," we should ask, "What should I say about the inner life? I have no ideas concerning what to speak. Please tell me something so that I may learn." The first brother may reply, "Perhaps you should say that the inner life is Christ." Then we can ask, "After I say that, what else should I speak?" In this way we should proceed point by point. This is the way I always dealt with Watchman Nee. I would even ask him how long my message should be. Brother Nee might say, "It is up to you," but I would reply, "I do not know how long to speak." If he suggested half an hour, I would finish my speaking within thirty minutes. Sometimes it took three hours to finish dealing with him in this way. I took the position that I truly did not know anything. In this way I learned very much. On one day I spent three hours learning, and on the next day I spent less than one hour speaking from what I had learned.

We must not only meet together, but we must learn. Many of you are younger and are smaller members. You may have some things, but the bigger members have more than you. Do not show off what you have; that does not help you to learn. You are here not for your teaching. You are here for learning. If you are going to show off what you have, then there is no need for you to learn more.

The messages in *The Normal Christian Church Life* were first given in 1937 beginning from the first day of the year. While we were in the north, we received a cable from Brother Nee asking us to come down to where he was. No further reason was given, so we just did what he asked. We took a train without a berth for thirty-six hours from Peking in the north to Shanghai in the south. When we arrived, Brother Nee came to the station to meet us. Right away he started to give the messages in that book. Those were not meetings but a conference of co-workers.

After about only two days, Brother Nee caught a heavy cold. He had a fever, so he could not rise up to come to the meeting. Early in the morning on the next day, Sister Nee came and asked me to contact Brother Nee. He was in bed, and I took a seat by him. He said, "Brother Lee, I cannot get up. You have to give a message on Acts 13." In the past two years he had covered the first part of the Acts from chapter one to chapter twelve. Now we had come to chapter thirteen, but he was unable to speak. I said, "What should I speak? What is in Acts 13?" He said, "You know," but I said, "I truly do not know. All I know is that there were prophets and teachers in the church in Antioch." He replied, "You have to tell the people about the line of Antioch." I said, "What is the line of Antioch?" Then he spoke to me concerning these matters.

When I went to speak, I said, "Brother Nee caught a cold, so he cannot come. He asked me to give you something, but I can only speak what he told me." Then I spoke about the line of Antioch from Acts 13. After two days Brother Nee rose up, came to the meeting, and gave the message on the line of Antioch again. I sat there and listened to it, saying to myself, "This is one hundred percent different from what I just spoke." He spoke something more, and I learned from him.

Due to Brother Nee's cold, the messages during those eight days in January were not given adequately. Then after the Japanese invaded China in July of the same year, we were forced to retreat from the coast to the interior. At that time I and some others were in north China, close to Mongolia, travelling and working. One day we received a cable summoning us down to Hankow in the center of China, on the Yangtze River, where the Chinese government was retreating to. At that time Brother Nee gave all those messages once again in an adequate way. *The Normal Christian Church Life* was published according to the long-hand notes taken there.

I always took the standing that I was learning. In order to learn something, we must be one hundred percent a learner. If we do this, we will see how much we will learn. We will learn more, and we will even learn the most.

Concerning our functioning in the church, there is the need of two sides. The bigger, older members must always take the stand not to replace others but to reproduce and perfect them, and the smaller, younger members must always take the stand to learn. If we care for these two sides, the functioning of the Body will be quick and adequate.

The poor situation in the church life, however, is that the bigger members do not reproduce and perfect, and the smaller ones do not learn. For the learners to criticize the bigger members for this poor situation does not help them. The learners should simply concentrate on learning. Then they will learn more. Suppose you teach me how to drive. If I am a good learner, I should not reason with you. If you tell me to drive on a certain road, I should not say that there is something in the way. I simply should take your orders. Then I will learn more.

These are the proper principles. In the church some are the older, bigger ones. This is something comparative. Someone may be a younger one to one person and an older one to another. I might be a smaller one to you, but I am a bigger one to someone else. As the younger ones, we have to learn, and as bigger ones, we have to reproduce and perfect others. I say again that we will see all the functions brought forth in an adequate, rich, and very fast way. These two principles are not a small matter.

GROWING UP INTO CHRIST IN ALL THINGS TO HAVE THE FULL GROWTH FOR OUR FUNCTION

We must also grow up into Christ in all things to have the full growth. Function depends on growth. Ephesians 4:13 speaks of arriving at a full-grown man. We need to have not a partial growth but the full growth until we become a full-grown man. Then verse 15 says that we grow up into Him in all things, who is the Head, Christ. This is to grow not merely in some things but in all things. This means that we may grow in certain things, but we may not have grown in other things. We need to grow up into Christ in all things.

Verse 14 says that we should no longer be little children tossed by waves and carried about by every wind of teaching. Darby's New Translation renders *children* as *babes*. If we are still babyish or childish, it is easy to be tossed by waves and carried about. How then can we function? Today in the church life only those who are established can function. The way to be established is by growth. If we are not established, we cannot function properly. We have to be established, but being established is possible only by growing.

Some may ask what they should do before they are grown up, while they are still babyish or childish, to escape from being carried about by every wind of teaching. What they must do is stay with the older ones. Consider children and babes. They are safe when they stay with their parents or their bigger brothers. Sometimes a mother brings some little ones, three or four years old, to the supermarket or a department store, and they get lost. The way for them not to get lost is to stay by their parents. Learn to stay with the older ones, and learn to grow. Then you will have a certain kind of function.

We need to grow up in everything into Christ. In certain things we already may have grown into Christ, but in other things we may not have the mature growth. How much we can function depends entirely on our growth. The more growth we have, the more function we have. We have to stress the matter of our growth. We have to minister life and nourishment to the brothers so that they may grow.

COORDINATION THROUGH THE MEASURE OF EACH ONE PART

Ephesians 4:16 implies the coordination of the Body. In this verse we do not have the word *coordination,* but we have the fact, the reality of it. Verse 16 says, "Out from whom all the Body, being joined together and being knit together through every joint of the rich supply and through the operation in the measure of each one part, causes the growth of the Body unto the building up of itself in love." *Out from whom* means out from the Head, Christ. This verse speaks of being joined together and knit together. It is not enough simply to be joined together. If I stack three books, they are joined together, but they are not knit together. Apparently we are in the church joined together, but we may not be knit together. Being knit together indicates the real building up. We must not only come together but be truly built up together. The apostle was careful to use the words *joined* and *knit* because there is a difference between them. If we come to gather together, but we have never been knit together, there is no building. What we have is only a pile of materials. We need not only to be brought together but also to be built up, knit together.

The whole body is joined together and knit together through every joint of the rich supply. In the body there are many joints, and all of these joints are the members of supply; they are stronger and richer. In the church some brothers and sisters are the joints. They are richer and stronger, so they are the members of the rich supply. They always supply something by ministering to all the members. It is by these supplying joints, these joints of supply, that the whole body is knit together. The joining and knitting is through the operation in the measure of each one part. This operation is the function of the members.

The coordination of the members is implied by the phrase *the operation in the measure of each one part.* If I function according to my measure, and everyone functions according to his measure, we will have the coordination. The operation in the measure of every part is the function of each member in coordination. If one member does not function, we are short of a measure. We all have to function in our proper measure, not too much or too little. When we each function in the proper measure, we have the coordination. The issue of this is the growth of the Body unto the building up of itself in love. It is by the function of life that the church is built up.

Through our fellowship at this time we all have been helped to be clear. However, we need much practice. Pray for these matters, and bring all this into practice in the place where you are. The more we fellowship in this way, the more we see the need for the real function of life. The real function comes from life, not from gift. As we have seen, in Romans the gift is the function given to the members, while in Ephesians the gift is the member given to the Body. The gifts in 1 Corinthians 12 are the miraculous gifts. These only help to lead us to life. The miraculous gifts themselves do not build up very much. Rather, they open the way to bring us into the reality of life. It is by the life supply that a certain function comes out. This causes us to become members qualified to build up the Body.

CHAPTER FIVE

THE PRODUCING OF THE GIFTS BY THE FLOW OF THE TRIUNE GOD IN THE DEATH, RESURRECTION, AND ASCENSION OF CHRIST

Scripture Reading: Psa. 68:18; 36:8; Eph. 4:11-12

The Amplified Bible renders Psalm 68:18 as, "You have ascended on high. You have led away captive a train of vanquished foes." We may also render the last phrase, "a host of vanquished foes." It was on the cross and by His resurrection that the Lord vanquished the foes, defeated them, and disarmed them. Then when He ascended to the heavens, He led a train, a parade, of defeated foes. In the ancient times, when a general went to war, gained the victory, and captured his foes, he returned victoriously with a train of defeated foes in a parade to show his victory. This is the thought in Psalm 68:18. Christ was the General who went to the battlefield and won the victory. He defeated the foes, disarmed them, and captured them. Then they became a parading train, a host, a defeated army, to show people what kind of victory the General had won. When Christ ascended on high to the heavens, He led away such a parade of defeated foes to show His victory and declare that all the negative things in the universe had been dealt with.

THE FLOW OF THE TRIUNE GOD

By this time we have gained more understanding concerning Christ's ascending on high. In the Triune God, the Father is the source, the Son is the course, and the Spirit is the flow within the course. This is the water of life. The Father is the source, the fountain, of living water. This source flows out through the Son, who is the course. In this course there is the flow of the river of life. This is the Triune God flowing out and flowing into us as life. This is not a human thought; this is the true revelation of the Word. Throughout the past twenty centuries, only a few Christian teachers here and there have touched this matter a little. Generally speaking, nearly all of Christianity has lost this concept and revelation. In these last days we have the inner sense of the moving Spirit that the Lord will recover this once more. Again and again the ministering Spirit has been striving to this end.

At the beginning of the Bible there was a flow beside the tree of life (Gen. 2:9-10). Then this flow is found throughout the entire Bible. In the Old Testament there is the smitten rock that flowed out the living water (Exo. 17:6), and there is the flow in Psalm 46:4, Ezekiel 47:1-12, and Zechariah 14:8. In the New Testament there is the flow of living water in John 4 and 7 and in 1 Corinthians 10 and 12. Verse 13 of chapter twelve says that we "were all given to drink one Spirit." This means that the Spirit is water to us. Eventually we come to Revelation 21 and 22, where we again see the flow. This flow is the water of life, which is God Himself.

In the Bible there are several portions that tell us that God is the fountain. Psalm 36:8 and 9 say, "They are saturated with the fatness of Your house, / And You cause them to drink of the river of Your pleasures. / For with You is the fountain of life." This verse speaks of both the river and the fountain. God is the living water to us; this is the divine concept, the divine thought.

THE FLOW PRODUCING
A UNIVERSAL MINGLING OF GOD AND MAN

The Father is the source, the Son is the course, and the Spirit is the flow within the course. I do want you to be impressed by this concept. *Hymns,* #12 says, "O God, Thou art the source of life." This source of life flows out in the Son and as the Spirit. Eventually this flow of living water—the Triune God in three persons—flows into us, the man of spirit, soul, and body. In Genesis 2:10 the river in the garden divided and became four branches. Four here represents man, meaning that this one river flows to this man and into man. From Himself as the source, God flows out and flows into man. This flowing out and flowing in eventually issues in a universal mingling of God with man. It is by this flow that God is brought into man, and it is also by this flow that man is brought into God. Therefore, the Lord said, "Abide in Me and I in you" (John 15:4). Who is this "Me?" It is God. To abide in Me means to abide in God. Who then is this "I?" It is also God. John 14:20 says, "In that day you will know that I am in My Father, and you in Me, and I in you." This is the mingling of God with man by the flow. I wish to make this very clear to you. This is something very basic concerning the inner life and the church life.

God Coming into Man

What do we call this flow when it comes down into man? It is the incarnation. By incarnation God has been brought into man. When a child was born in Bethlehem to the human race, something very extraordinary happened. Isaiah 9:6 says "For a child is born to us, / A son is given to us; / And the government / Is upon His shoulder; / And His name will be called Wonderful Counselor, / Mighty God, / Eternal Father, / Prince of Peace." A child was born in a manger, yet His name is called Mighty God. It is by this incarnation that God has been brought into man. In the four Gospels there was a man working on this earth having God in Him as His very content. This is a wonder and a mystery. At that time this wonder was a secret to the people, because apparently this was simply a man, Jesus. However, there was something within Him that was different from men, that is, God. By His incarnation God brought Himself into man.

Man Being Brought into God

Later Christ resurrected and ascended, and by the resurrection and ascension man was brought into God. Therefore, after the ascension there is a man in the heavens. At the time Stephen was stoned to death, the heavens were opened to him, and he saw the Son of Man at the right hand of God (Acts 7:55-56). That man in the heavens was not only in heaven

but also in God. Stephen saw a man in God. By the incarnation there was a man on this earth with God in Him. God
came into man and walked on this earth. At that time someone could point to Him and say that there is God in a man. By
His resurrection and ascension, however, there is now a man
in God. This is wonderful! God has been brought into man,
and man has been brought into God.

Psalm 68:18 first says, "You have ascended on high," and
then it says, "You have led captive those taken captive." When
did Christ defeat all His foes? Hebrews 2:14 tells us that
through death He destroyed him—the devil—who has the
power of death. By His death Christ defeated all the foes.
Then by His resurrection He disarmed them. After this, while
He was ascending to the heavens, He was leading a train of
defeated foes. Do you realize this? Christ has disarmed and
captured all the capturing power, and He has defeated all the
foes. He has solved all the problems in the heavens and on
the earth.

CHRIST GOING TO THE FATHER
IN RESURRECTION AND ASCENSION
TO RECEIVE MEN AS GIFTS

Christ went not only to the heavens but to the Father
Himself. The Gospel of John tells us that Jesus came from the
Father and was going to the Father (13:1, 3; 14:12). He came
from the Father to bring God into man, and then He went to
the Father to bring man into God. Psalm 68:18 says that
Christ received gifts among, in, or as, man. Christ is a man. In
this man, as man, representing man, for man, and on behalf
of man He went back to the Father to receive the gifts. These
gifts are all the members.

Do not merely take my word. You must read the clear word
of God. Ephesians 4:8 says, "Therefore the Scripture says,
'Having ascended to the height, He led captive those taken
captive and gave gifts to men.'" Verses 9 and 10 are a paren-
thesis, so verse 8 is followed by verse 11, which says, "And He
Himself gave some as apostles and some as prophets and some
as evangelists and some as shepherds and teachers." Here
Christ did not give speaking in tongues, healing, wonders,

power, and miracles. Rather, He gave persons as gifts for the perfecting of the saints. The gifts are not only the apostles, prophets, evangelists, and shepherds and teachers. Not only are the arm and the shoulder gifts to the body; even the little finger is a gift to the body. The gifts are the members.

According to Psalm 68, Christ ascended on high, having defeated and disarmed the foes by His death and resurrection. By His incarnation, death, resurrection, and ascension, Christ accomplished everything both negatively and positively. On the negative side, He solved all the problems, defeated all the foes, and led them as a train of defeated foes to show His victory to the whole universe. On the positive side, He brought God into man and man into God. Everything is now accomplished. At the time of His ascension, He was ready as a man, in man, and on behalf of man to receive the gifts back from the Father, the source. These gifts are the members of His Body.

THE MEMBERS BEING PRODUCED
AS GIFTS TO THE BODY

Christ's producing of the members for His Body was His receiving of the gifts from the Father, because the Father is the source. At the same time, this receiving of the members was also the giving of the members to the Body as gifts. The producing was the receiving, and the receiving was the giving.

Where are we? We are included in this producing, this receiving, and this giving. We are the members of the Body, and since we are members, we are gifts to the Body. If a certain brother were not a gift to the Body, the church in his locality never would have come into existence. The gifts, as members of the Body, were produced by the flowing out and flowing back of the Triune God. This producing started on the day of resurrection and was accomplished on the day of Pentecost. We all were produced as members on the day of resurrection and the day of Pentecost. Paul, Peter, James, John, you, and I were all produced at the same time.

When were you saved? You have to say, "At the same time that Peter was saved. When Peter was saved, I was saved." The crossing of the Red Sea is a type of this fact. All the people of Israel were saved through the Passover and the crossing of the Red Sea. It was not that Moses crossed the Red Sea at one time, and the rest of Israel crossed many years later. In the eyes of God, the whole of Israel, including the great and the small, held the Passover and crossed the Red Sea at the same time. With God there is no limitation of time. Likewise, by the resurrection and ascension of Christ, we all were produced as members, that is, as gifts. These members were received by the Father, because He is the source. Then the Son as the Head of the Body received the members from the Father as the source. This was the producing of the members. At the same time, all these members were given to the Body as gifts. Therefore, the producing was the receiving, and the receiving was the giving. While to the Father and the Son it was a giving, to the Body it was a receiving.

BECOMING MEMBERS OF THE UNIVERSAL MINGLING
BY THE ALL-INCLUSIVE DOSE
OF THE TRIUNE GOD COMING INTO US

Now we can see where we are and how we were produced. It was through Christ's incarnation, death, resurrection, and ascension all the way to our regeneration that we the fallen men were made members of the Body. To regenerate is to produce a member from a fallen man. What kind of man is the fallen man? Sin is in his body (Rom. 7:23), the self is in his soul (Matt. 16:24-26; Luke 9:23-25), and death is in his spirit (Eph. 2:1, 5; Col. 2:13). The soul became the evil self when it became independent of God. Moreover, fallen man is dead not in the body or in the soul but in the spirit. Before we were saved, when we were living in the body and very active in the soul, we were dead in our spirit. In such a condition, our whole being was under darkness, that is, under the power of Satan.

How could such a person be made a member of Christ? It is by the all-inclusive dose coming into him. When this all-inclusive dose comes in, it brings the element of Christ's death to dissolve sin, self, and death, and it also brings the resurrection power to free us. This is on the negative side. On the positive side, this dose contains the incarnation that brought God into man and the ascension that brought man into God. This produced a mingling, and this mingling has come into us to regenerate us and to make us a part of the universal mingling. This universal mingling is the Head with the Body, which ultimately is the New Jerusalem. Therefore, to be a part of the universal mingling is to be a member of the Body. We all have been made a part, members, of this mingling.

All the negative things—sin, self, death, Satan, and darkness—have been solved and dissolved, the mingling of God with man has been brought into us, and we have been made a part of this mingling. This means that we have been made a member of this universal man, the universal mingling of God with man. This mingling has been injected into us, so we have become members, and these members are gifts given to the Body. Strictly speaking, it was not Saul of Tarsus who was a gift; it was Paul. Therefore, we all have to change our muddy, earthy "name"; that is, we all have to be transformed.

Now we are clearer about Psalm 68:18, and we have a newer understanding of the ascension. The meaning of the ascension is that man has been brought into God by incarnation, but this is only half of the mingling of God and man. When Christ ascended to the heavens, He brought man into God. By this, the mingling is now complete. Everything has been accomplished. Everything has been done on both the negative and positive sides. Now this all-inclusive dose comes into us to produce the members, to make us the members of the Body, to take those who were received from the Father and give them to the Body as gifts. If our eyes are opened to see all these things, this will be a real release and delivery to us. There is no need to struggle to overcome our failures or to apply the cross to ourselves. If we have the vision that everything on the negative side has been dealt with and everything on the positive side is ours, we will be released.

THE MEMBERS BEING PRODUCED FOR THE PURPOSE OF THE BUILDING UP OF GOD'S DWELLING

Psalm 68:18 concludes with: "You have received gifts among

men, / Even the rebellious ones also, / That Jehovah God may dwell among them." The purpose for the producing of the members, the receiving of the gifts, and the giving of the gifts to the Body is the building up of the dwelling place of God on this earth among men. All this is for the building up of the Body. This completely corresponds with the thought in Ephesians 4. Verses 11 and 12 say, "And He Himself gave some as apostles and some as prophets and some as evangelists and some as shepherds and teachers, for the perfecting of the saints unto the work of the ministry, unto the building up of the Body of Christ." The Body of Christ is the dwelling place of God on this earth among men.

THE BUILDING UP OF THE CHURCH
BEING ACCOMPLISHED ONLY
BY THE FLOWING OF THE TRIUNE GOD

In the past few years I have heard people speak of forming a "New Testament church." I have the feeling that many of these dear brothers are speaking about something that they do not understand. The church is not formed in this way. The church is produced by the flow of the Triune God with the incarnation, crucifixion, resurrection, and ascension. When this flow comes into us, the all-inclusive dose is applied to us. Then sin, self, death, darkness, Satan, the world, and the other negative things are all dissolved. Moreover, all that God is and all that man is are brought into us to produce us, to make us members of the Body. It is in this flow that we become proper, living members given to the Body. When we are living in this flow, we are transformed and we are built up. Then we have the reality of the church, the reality of the Body.

Consider church history and our situation today. People have written many books about the church, and they talk much about the Body life and the "New Testament church." Please tell me, though, where is such a church? There is not such a church today because people do not experience this flow. If we brothers and sisters here do not realize this flow, then regardless of how much we talk about the church life and the Body life, we still will not have it, and we will not be able to have it. The Body does not come from talking; it comes from the flowing.

This is why in these past two and a half years my burden has been to stress this matter. We must have the flow of the Triune God with His incarnation, crucifixion, resurrection, and ascension to bring God into man and to bring man into God that we may be fully transformed. It is by this that we can practice the building up of the Body. The formula that I have presented here did not "come from the sky." This formula has been proved by use for more than thirty-five years. I assure you that it is truly workable. Only the flow matters, and only this flow works.

When we had the first training in Taiwan ten years ago, I stressed the same matters. There is no need to pass something else on to you. This flow alone is good enough. The flow solves all the problems, and it meets all the needs. Moreover, this flow is for the purpose of the building, so that the Lord God may dwell among men. We have to pray for this matter that the Lord may bring more and more seeking and wandering ones into this reality. Without this understanding, there is no place for the seeking ones to go, and there is no hope for them to rest. In addition, there is no hope of a dwelling place for God, a place for the Lord to rest on the earth today. This is the only way, and this is the only hope. In John 14:2 and 4 the Lord Jesus said, "In My Father's house are many abodes; if it were not so, I would have told you; for I go to prepare a place for you....And where I am going you know the way." The place and the way He spoke of are in the flow of the Triune God to produce His dwelling.

Until the Lord's children, the seeking ones and wandering ones, are brought into this realization, they can never have rest. They are still in the wandering process, and God is homeless among them. Therefore, we must pray for them. This is not a movement, an organization, or something formed by man. Rather, this is a matter of the flow of life. It is by this flow that the real building up of the Body will be realized. The Lord promised that He would come quickly, but two thousand years have passed, and He is still not here. This is due to the lack of the realization of the flow.

It is by the flow that the bride will be prepared and adorned (Rev. 21:2). I do not have the assurance that the whole church will be prepared as the bride. According to the revelation of the New Testament, it will not be so. However, I do believe that at least a minority, a small number of the saints, will be brought back to the flow. This minority will be the ones who bring Christ back. This is similar to the type in the Old Testament. It was not the majority of the Jews who brought in Christ's first coming. It was only that remnant who came back to the Holy Land. Although they may have been in a weak condition, it was still they who brought in Christ the first time. Many thousands of Jews were scattered in many places, some even in large communities, but Christ was not born among them. Rather, Christ was born among the small number who came back to the Holy Land.

The second coming of Christ will be the same in principle as His first coming. If a small remnant will come back to the original ground and standing, they will bring Christ back. This is the Lord's recovery. This is not a movement, an organization, something formed by man, teachings, or gifts. This is simply the flow of life. We all have to be brought into this flow of life, and we have to pray about this. Whenever we go to the Lord to pray about this matter, we are alive and living within, and we sense the inner flow, the anointing. This proves that the Lord is desirous to have this recovery.

This is His move, not our movement. If we will forget about our own needs, our family problems, and even other people's needs and simply remember the Lord's need for this flow of life, and if we will pray for this, right away we will sense the flowing and the anointing within. We will be enlivened, because this is something that the Lord desires. He is seeking after this flow. Again I say, this is not any kind of teaching, gift, organization, or formation. This is simply the flow of life. This is what the Lord is seeking after, because it is only by this that His purpose can be fulfilled, His goal can be attained, and His bride can be prepared. The Lord has now begun this work.

CHAPTER SIX

THE HOLY PRIESTHOOD
AND THE ROYAL PRIESTHOOD
TO MINISTER THE VARIED GRACE OF GOD

Scripture Reading: 1 Pet. 2:2-9; 4:10-11

The First Epistle of Peter gives us several important items related to the service of the church. The first item is the believers' birth as newborn babes. This is referred to as regeneration in 1:3: "Blessed be the God and Father of our Lord Jesus Christ, who according to His great mercy has regenerated us unto a living hope through the resurrection of Jesus Christ from the dead." Then verse 23 says, "Having been regenerated not of corruptible seed but of incorruptible, through the living and abiding word of God." The divine birth means everything to us. Second, after birth there is growth. Verse 2 of chapter two says, "As newborn babes, long for the guileless milk of the word in order that by it you may grow unto salvation." Third, the way to grow is by feeding on the Lord, which includes tasting Him (v. 3). If we have ever tasted the Lord, we will want to feed on Him. Feeding on Him implies the preciousness of the Lord (v. 4). The worldly people disallow and reject the Lord, but we treasure Him. We realize His preciousness, so we feed on Him by tasting Him. The fourth main item is the building (v. 5a). It is by feeding that we grow, and it is by growth that we have the building.

The fifth important matter in 1 Peter is the priestly service, the priesthood (vv. 5b, 9). This priesthood is the service, a matter of function. This depends on the building, the building depends on growth, and growth comes from the birth. Therefore, the priestly service is a matter of life. We have to stress again that without the inner life and the growth of life, the church life is not possible. John deals with regeneration, Paul deals with the inner life, and Peter deals with the same matters. The first chapter of 1 Peter speaks of being regenerated through the resurrection of Christ and by the living word of God as the seed sown into us. This is the beginning of the inner life, and this is also the beginning of the priesthood, the service. Service comes from life.

GROWING BY FEEDING ON THE LORD

The growth of life is the expanding, the spreading, of the inner life. Again we must consider the spirit, soul, and body. John 3:6b says, "That which is born of the Spirit is spirit." We were born of the Holy Spirit in our spirit. Now the growth of life is the spreading of this life to all the parts of our soul. In 1 Peter we see the relationship between the spirit and the soul. Verse 22a of chapter one says, "You have purified your souls." The purification of our souls was accomplished after our regeneration. Verse 23 speaks of regeneration, which is in the spirit and comes before the purifying of the soul. After the rebirth in the spirit we need the purification of the soul. Our soul has three parts. In the mind are the old thoughts; in the emotion are old, rotten, evil things; and in the will is rebellion. Therefore, our soul needs purifying. This purifying mentioned by Peter is equal to the transformation spoken of by Paul. The purifying of the soul is the transformation of the soul. Regeneration is the birth, and transformation is the growth, the spreading of life within to permeate, saturate, and purify our soul.

This growth is made possible only by our feeding on the Lord. Verse 2 of chapter two says that we drink the guileless milk of the word, and verse 3 says that we taste the Lord. Verse 4 begins, "Coming to Him." To come to the Lord is not once for all. This coming must be continual. We have to come to the Lord again and again, and the reason we do this is that we sense that the Lord is precious. He is dear, sweet, and precious to us. We just like to come to Him and contact Him. I like the phrase *coming to Him*. The more we come to Him, the more we feed on Him. In 1 Peter 2, we have the drinking of the milk, the tasting of the Lord, and the continual coming to

Him. We treasure Him. He is gracious, sweet, dear, and precious to us, so we simply like to come to Him. Then the more we come to Him, the more we drink of Him, feed on Him, and take Him in. It is by this contact with the Lord that we grow.

BEING TRANSFORMED INTO LIVING STONES

This growth by feeding on the Lord causes us to be transformed into living stones. Originally, we were not living stones; we were merely clay, something made of earth and dust. However, here it says we are living stones. This is due to transformation. God's building throughout all the Scriptures is always with stones. God's building is never built with bricks. The city and tower of Babel as well as the two treasure cities of Pharaoh were built with bricks. Bricks are formed of the dust, the constituent of our natural life. Genesis 2:7 says that we were made with dust, and 1 Corinthians 15:47 tells us that "the first man, Adam, is out of the earth, earthy." Second Corinthians 4:7 also tells us that we are the earthen vessels. Bricks signify something formed of the natural life. Satan builds up his building with the human natural life.

In God's building there are only stones, not bricks. Therefore, we must be regenerated and have a change in nature to be no longer natural. Second, we need to be transformed from something earthly into something spiritual. All our natural concepts, natural energy, and natural elements must be transformed. When bricks are made from clay, they are formed but not transformed. To produce stones, however, the clay must be not merely formed but transformed. It is by transformation that we have the living stones as the material for the building. The way to have this transformation is by feeding on Christ. By feeding on Christ we have growth, and this growth causes us to be transformed. The more we feed on Christ, the more we grow in Him, and the more we grow in Him, the more we are transformed. We must have neither an American concept nor a Chinese concept. All our natural concepts must be transformed to be the spiritual, divine, and heavenly concepts. The natural life, the muddy life, the life of clay, has to be transformed into stone.

GROWTH AND TRANSFORMATION
BEING NECESSARY FOR THE BUILDING UP

Without growth and transformation, there is no possibility of building. In many places I have observed that a sister may be very good, nice, humble, and sweet and have much love in the natural life. The church may even commit significant responsibilities to her. After only a few weeks, however, this sister may be influenced by a number of small matters to stop coming to the meetings. In the same way, a brother who was so good last year may be in worldly pursuits this year. We may compare this goodness to a building of clay. The clay appears to be very solid, but if water is poured on it, the clay falls apart, and there is a hole in the building. Anything built of clay cannot stand against water. However, if water is poured on a piece of marble, it only cleans the marble. The more the water is poured on the marble, the more the marble becomes clean. Are we marble or clay like an adobe house? If we are marble, any kind of rain that falls on us will only cleanse us and make us more shining. However, if we are clay, we will be washed away. After only two months we will disappear from the meetings. People talk much about the church life, but without growth and transformation there can be no church life.

This is why we must once again stress the need for the inner life and the growth. Without the inner life and the growth, there is no possibility to have the church life. Regardless of what we build up, it will be a building of mud, clay, wood, grass, and stubble, not of stones. It will not be able to stand any kind of test. The building comes from transformation and growth.

A certain spiritual co-worker in China was arrested by the Communists and put into prison. The Communists were not able to accuse him of anything, so they simply asked him to say two things: that as a mere human Watchman Nee was not perfect and could be mistaken, and that the church also was not perfect and had shortcomings. If the brother would say this little word, he would have been released right away. However, he would not say it. The Communists then worked on his wife who, as a weaker vessel, was more or less convinced by them. She then was brought to the prison to speak with her husband to convince him. The brother told his wife, "I cannot say anything like this in order to save my life. If the Spirit within me leads me to say this, I will say it. If not, I will not say it simply to save my life." Then the Communists worked on his son to do the same thing. After the son's first talk with him, the brother would not listen to him, and the son was unable to do anything. No one could shake the brother or move him. Eventually his kidneys degenerated, and he died. This brother was strong in his spiritual character, like a piece of marble. He was trustworthy, and no one could change him. The church can be built up with this kind of material, a strong, transformed character, not one like a piece of clay. The real building of the church requires this kind of stone, this kind of material transformed by growth.

How much responsibility the church can assign to certain brothers or sisters depends on how much transformation they have. Without transformation, a person is not trustworthy. We cannot trust in someone if his person is muddy. Today he may be good, but tomorrow he may be gone. The building of the church is possible only by transformation through the growth of life. This is why in 1 Peter 1 and 2 we have birth, growth, transformation, and the material for the building, in that order.

THE BUILT-UP PRIESTHOOD
IN ITS HOLY AND KINGLY ASPECTS

Then after the building, there is the priesthood. First Peter 2:5a says, "You yourselves also, as living stones, are being built up as a spiritual house into a holy priesthood." What is this spiritual house? It is a holy priesthood. The priesthood itself is the building, the house. This means that we become a serving body. A priest is a serving person, but this verse speaks not merely of a serving person but a serving company, a serving body, a serving group of people. It is when we are built together that we have the adequate service; that is, the adequate service, the adequate function, comes from the genuine building up. When we are built together, we are able to serve. In other words, the service is the building, and the priesthood is the house. If we are the built-up house, we are the serving body, the priesthood.

This priesthood has two aspects. Verse 5 speaks of the holy priesthood, while verse 9 speaks of the royal priesthood, the kingly priesthood. There are two orders of priests mentioned in the Bible, the order of Aaron and the order of Melchisedec. The order of Aaron is the holy priesthood, and the order of Melchisedec is the royal, kingly priesthood. Melchisedec was a kingly priest, a king as well as a priest (Heb. 7:1). To be holy is to be one who is separated unto God and goes to God with a burden for people. When Aaron went in to God, he bore the names of the twelve tribes on his shoulders and on his breast (Exo. 28:9-12, 15-21), that is, in power and in love. He was separated from the common people unto God, and he brought people to God. As such, he was the holy priest. The kingly priest is exemplified by Melchisedec. At the time Melchisedec met him, Abraham had been fighting the battle, and he needed bread and wine to refresh him. Melchisedec came out from God with bread and wine to meet Abraham's need (Gen. 14:17-18). These are the two directions of the priests. The holy priest goes to God with man's need. The kingly priest comes out of God and goes to man with the supply, the bread and wine, to meet his need. The real service of the church is always in these two aspects.

We may illustrate these two aspects of the priesthood by our gospel preaching. Before a week of preaching the gospel, we may spend a week for prayer. In this way we bear our burden to the Lord, praying day by day in the presence of the Lord. This is the service of the holy priesthood. Then after our prayer, we come out from the presence of the Lord with bread and wine to minister to others to meet their need. At this time we become the royal, kingly priesthood. This is the principle of the service. In order to have the real priestly service, the real priesthood, we need the building up as the basis, and we need to go to the Lord as holy priests to contact Him. Then from His presence we come out with something of Himself as the bread and the wine to minister to others to meet their need. This is the real service of the church.

If the built-up priesthood is holy and is also kingly, we have the proper service. This requires the adequate building up, the adequate contacting of the Lord, and the adequate ministering of bread and wine from the Lord to others. What we minister to others as the kingly priests is not merely teaching; it must be bread and wine, which are the riches of the Lord ministered to others through us. This is the proper principle of the service.

It seems that 1 Peter 2:5 through 9 is a short and simple portion of the Word, but all the principles of the service are here. These are the principles of rebirth, feeding, growth, transformation, building up, the holy priesthood, and the kingly priesthood. By all these we have the ministry of life and the proper, adequate function and service of the church.

BEING GOOD STEWARDS
OF THE VARIED GRACE OF GOD

In chapter four of 1 Peter there is one more principle related to service. Verse 10 says, "Each one, as he has received a gift, ministering it among yourselves as good stewards of the varied grace of God." The principle here is that all the gifts are for ministering grace to others. The gifts in 1 Peter 4 are the same kind of gifts that are in Romans 12. These gifts are the various functions. We all have received gifts—that is, we all have received functions—because we all are members. With every member there is a function as a gift given to that member. According to 1 Peter 4:10, we all have received a gift. Now we have to exercise the gift, using it to minister the varied grace of God to others.

Many times we extend hospitality to others. This extending of hospitality is a gift. However, what we are doing is not only the giving of hospitality. By extending hospitality we become stewards of the varied grace of God. By extending hospitality we minister grace, which is Christ as life, to our guests. However, it is possible to extend hospitality without ministering life. Too many times we give hospitality, but instead of ministering life we minister death. If morning and evening we merely pass on gossip to our guests, we are ministering death; this is a killing. Instead of supplying grace, we supply germs. Our function is not merely to do things, but by doing these things we minister Christ as grace to others. Those who are ushers in the meetings minister Christ to others by their ushering. Those who clean the meeting hall not only clean, but by their cleaning they minister Christ as life and grace. We all have received a gift so that we may be the good stewards of the varied grace of God.

I observed a sister in China who did nothing but wash clothes for our guests. Simply by that washing, this sister ministered life all the time. Anyone who contacted her through her washing of clothes had the sense that life was ministered to him. This is the principle of the genuine service. The unique principle concerning service in 1 Peter 4 is that all the functions are not merely to do a job but to minister Christ as life and grace to others.

In 1948 a wonderful revival took place among us in Shanghai. One day during this time, the church had a love feast. One serving sister among us was able to do everything very nicely, but at that time she did not minister life. People could sense her ability and intelligence, but that frustrated the life. There was another sister who was serving there, who while she was serving, dropped a bowl on the ground. She made a mistake, yet by her attitude and her spirit, we could sense the flow of life. In terms of business, the first sister was good, and the second sister was poor. In terms of life, however, the second sister had the flow of life. She broke a bowl, but life was flowing through her. We all have to learn to minister Christ as grace and life to others by exercising our gift, our function. As we function, as we are doing a certain job, we have to minister life to others.

Verse 11 continues, "If anyone speaks, as speaking oracles of God; if anyone ministers, as ministering out of the strength which God supplies; that in all things God may be glorified through Jesus Christ, to whom is the glory and the might forever and ever. Amen." Again, the principle here is that we minister grace to others. We must pray about these matters and bring them to the Lord.

CHAPTER SEVEN

THE PRIESTHOOD

(1)

Scripture Reading: 1 Pet. 2:5, 9

In order to see what the function of the divine life is, we have to see more concerning the priesthood. The priesthood is a very important matter in the Scriptures. We must consider what a priest is, what the life of a priest is, and what the function of a priest is. Moreover, we may ask who were the first priests in the Bible, who are the last priests, and what is the difference between a priest, a king, and a prophet. Last, we must ask what the relationship is between the priesthood and the image and authority of God. If we can find out these seven matters, we will be deeply impressed with the priesthood. This has very much to do with our function as Christians. Many Christians today do not function properly mostly due to their lack in apprehending these seven points.

WHAT A PRIEST IS

One Who Serves God with Christ

It is not sufficient to say that a priest is simply a person who serves God. Rather, we must say that a priest is a person who serves God through Christ as the reality of the offerings (Lev. 1—7). A Gentile priest is one who serves God without Christ, but a genuine priest of God is one who serves God with Christ, through Christ, and by Christ.

One Who Enjoys Christ

Moreover, a priest is a person who enjoys Christ. The priests eat what they offer as the sacrifices. The serving ones serve God with Christ and through Christ, and they enjoy Christ. The offerings in Leviticus are for the enjoyment both of God and of the offering priest. The burnt offering was wholly burnt unto God; nothing was left as a share for the priest (Lev. 1:3, 9). However, the greater part of the meal offering was for the enjoyment of the priest (2:1-3; 6:16-18). Of the peace offering, the greater parts, the breast and the right thigh, were to be eaten by the priests (7:34). The right thigh signifies strength, and the breast signifies love. Both of these parts as a heave offering and wave offering were for the enjoyment of the priest. Likewise, part of the sin offering and trespass offering were for God, but much of them was to be eaten by the offering priest (6:25-26; 7:1, 6).

One Who Lives By Christ

A priest is also a person who lives by Christ. His eating is Christ, his clothing is Christ, and his dwelling is Christ. People today always speak of eating, clothing, and housing. A priest, however, eats the offerings, that is, Christ. In addition, every item of the priests clothing signifies Christ. They truly put on Christ as their clothing. Their dwelling place is the tabernacle, which also signifies Christ. Therefore, their eating, clothing, housing, and their everything is Christ.

One Who Contacts God in the Mingling with God

A priest is a person who contacts God in the mingling with God. The priest's passing through the Holy Place and into the Holy of Holies is his contact with God, and this contact is not in himself but in a mingling with God. A priest's contact with God is in God. That is, as he contacts God, he is mingled with God, not objectively but subjectively. This is very deep. Today as the priests, when we go to contact God, we contact Him not merely objectively but also subjectively. We do not contact God apart from God; we contact God in God, that is, in the mingling with God. The whole atmosphere within the tabernacle is God. Therefore, when the priest goes into the tabernacle, he is in God to contact God, and God is also in Him. We may compare this to contacting air. We do not contact air as we would a book. Instead, we contact the air by being in the air. Moreover, the air is also in us, so we are mingled with the air. Likewise, if we jump into a stream and take it in, we are covered by the water, and we are also filled with the water. Similarly, we contact God in the mingling with God.

One Who Is Absolutely and Thoroughly Mingled with God

A priest is one who is absolutely and thoroughly mingled with God. Everything in the atmosphere of the tabernacle, including the smoke, flavor, and substance of the offerings, signifies an aspect of God. For the priest to come into the tabernacle signifies a person coming into God. Once the priest is in the tabernacle, the atmosphere, the flavor, and even the shekinah glory gets into him, producing a mingling of the priest with God. When Moses stayed in such a condition with God for forty days and forty nights, he was shining (Exo. 34:28-30). God shined out through him because he was mingled with God.

One Who Becomes a Part of God's House

A priest is a person who becomes a part of God's dwelling, God's house. In the New Testament, in 1 Peter 2, we see that the house of God is the priesthood composed of all the priests (v. 5). Therefore, every priest is an item of the material for the building of the house. When a priest is mingled with God, spontaneously he becomes a part of the house of God. Eventually, Peter became a part of the New Jerusalem as one of its foundations (Rev. 21:14). Every redeemed and transformed one is a part of the New Jerusalem.

To be transformed by God is to be mingled with God. If I put some tea into a glass of plain water, the water will be mingled with the tea. Originally it was plain water, but now it is mingled with the tea. This mingling is transformation. The plain water is transformed into the nature, form, color, and flavor of the tea. We are the "plain water," and God is the "tea" put into us to mingle with us. The more God mingles with us, the more we are transformed into His nature, "color," "form," and "flavor." In this way we become a part of His dwelling place.

One Who Bears the Testimony of God

A priest also is a person who bears the testimony of God. To bear the testimony of God is not merely objective, as when the priests bore the ark in the Old Testament. Having passed through the six previous points, we can see that to bear the testimony means that we ourselves become a part of the testimony. To bear the real ark, the testimony of God, is not merely to carry it objectively; it is to be mingled with the ark subjectively as part of the ark.

One Who Ministers Christ to Others

A priest is one who ministers Christ to others. If we are a part of Christ, then whatever we minister is Christ. We are filled with Christ, covered with Christ, one with Christ, and mingled with Christ, so whatever we pass on, share, and minister to others is Christ—not knowledge, forms, or anything else. Water that is mingled with tea bears the testimony of the tea. This is a subjective testimony. Even one drop of this drink contains tea, because it is mingled with the tea. Likewise, if we are mingled with Christ, whatever we give to others has Christ in it.

In the service of the priests, whatever the priest shared with people signified an aspect of Christ. When a person of Israel brought an offering to the priest, the priest offered it to God. This was his priestly service. Then after making this offering, the priest passed on a portion to the offerer. This signifies passing on something of Christ to people. When the priest went into the Holy Place or the Holy of Holies, he enjoyed Christ in a fuller way, even in the fullest way. Then he had something even more of Christ to share with others. Whatever he brought out from the presence of God was a portion of Christ. This is a shadow, a picture, of our experience today.

One Who Brings Man into Fellowship with God and God into Fellowship with Man

A priest is one who brings man into fellowship with God and God into fellowship with man. The more the priests serve—whether by offering the sacrifices, arranging the bread of the Presence, lighting the lamps, or burning the incense—the more they bring people into the presence and fellowship of God. Then they bring something of God to the people, either a message, an instruction, or some item of God to minister to the people.

It is through the priest that there is the fellowship between God and His people and the fellowship among God's people. The fellowship depends absolutely upon the priesthood. Consider the picture in the Old Testament. If we were to take away the priesthood, then there would have been no fellowship between God and His people and no fellowship among His people. When we have the priesthood, we have this fellowship in two aspects: the fellowship of the people with God and the fellowship of the people among themselves. This one fellowship in two aspects is a matter of the priesthood. If we have the priesthood, we have the fellowship. If we do not have the priesthood, we do not have the fellowship.

Today it is the same in the church. The more priesthood we have, the more fellowship we have. If there is no priesthood, there is no spiritual fellowship. In today's Christianity there is a certain amount of friendship, but there is not much genuine fellowship because there is very little priesthood. The fellowship depends upon the priesthood.

One Who Builds Up the Dwelling Place of God

Lastly, a priest is a person who builds up the dwelling place of God. The priesthood was necessary for the building up of the tabernacle and later for the building of the temple and the recovery of the temple. Christ is the Builder of the temple with the priesthood. Zechariah 6:12 and 13 say, "And speak to him, saying, Thus speaks Jehovah of hosts, saying, Here is a man, whose name is the Shoot; and He will shoot forth from His place and will build the temple of Jehovah. Indeed, it is He who will build the temple of Jehovah; and He will bear majesty and will sit and rule on His throne; and He will be a priest on His throne; and the counsel of peace will be between the two of them." The man whose name is the Shoot is Christ. As the Builder of God's temple, He needed to

be the Priest. This shows us that it is the priesthood that
builds up the temple of God.

THE LIFE OF THE PRIESTS

Christ is also the life of the priests. The tree of life signifies that God is our enjoyment in Christ as the Holy Spirit
(Gen. 2:9; John 10:10b). The person who enjoys Christ the
most is the priest. What the priests are and what the priests
put on is Christ. Their clothing is Christ, and their dwelling
place is Christ. In those forty years in the wilderness, the
people of Israel enjoyed manna. The priests, however, enjoyed
a richer portion of Christ day by day. The people enjoyed a
simple, small portion of manna, but the priests day by day,
even in the wilderness, enjoyed the offerings as a richer, fuller
portion of Christ in His different aspects. Many people in
today's Christianity appreciate the manna, but the enjoyment
of manna is a sign of wandering. Those who enjoy manna are
in the wilderness, not in the rest or in the tabernacle. Those
who are in the tabernacle enjoy not merely manna but all
the riches of the offerings, even in the wilderness. Today the
majority of the church are like the people of Israel in the wilderness. However, a minority, a small number, are like the
priests, enjoying Christ in a fuller way in the tabernacle.

That Christ is the life of the priests is indicated by their
clothing. All the elements of the tabernacle are on the clothing of the priests. The tabernacle is covered with linen, and
the robes of the priest are made of linen. Within the tabernacle
is gold, and on the robes of the priest there is gold to hold the
precious stones (Exo. 28:5-8, 15-21). This signifies that every
aspect and item of the clothing of the priests are portions of
Christ. On the breastplate of the robe there are twelve stones
with the names of the twelve tribes, indicating that the twelve
tribes are transformed into precious stones, held by the gold,
and built up together. In the flow of the river in Genesis 2
there was onyx, a precious stone, and on the shoulder pieces of
the priest's robe are two onyx stones (Gen. 2:12; Exo. 28:9-12).
The priests have Christ as their righteousness, signified
by the white linen; Christ as their sanctification, signified by
the gold; and Christ as their transformation, signified by the

precious stones. They also have Christ as their glorification, signified by the shining of the stones, and Christ as their building up, signified by the twelve stones built together in the gold settings. All these are different aspects of Christ. The eating, clothing, housing, and everything in the life of the priests are Christ.

THE FUNCTION OF THE PRIESTS

The function of the priests is always to minister Christ either to man or to God. When they offer the sacrifices, they minister Christ to God. When they share the sacrifices with the people, they minister Christ to the people. The key point of the function of the priests, however, is not to offer sacrifices but to burn the incense. According to Exodus and Leviticus, the priests were charged to burn the incense as their central service. Then whenever they burn the incense, they also have to light the lamps of the lampstand and set the bread of the Presence.

Our function today is to burn the incense. This is not merely to pray but to offer the resurrected Christ to God in prayer. When we come together in the meeting, we do not mainly offer the sacrifices. Rather, the main thing we do is offer the incense. When we come together to meet, are we in the outer court or in the Holy Place? The meeting for preaching the gospel is a meeting in the outer court, but Christian meetings such as the prayer meeting and the Lord's table meeting are in the Holy Place. In these meetings we offer the incense, that is, the resurrected Christ, to God in our prayer. By doing this, at the same time we light the lamps. As we offer prayer with the incense, people are enlightened. At the same time also we set the bread of the Presence upon the table to feed people.

In the past we have said that we offer Christ as the offerings in the meetings. This is still true. The younger ones among us offer the Lord as the offerings. The more experienced ones, however, offer the Lord as the incense. Do you like to offer the offerings, or do you like to offer the incense? We would rather offer the incense. However, we cannot pretend to do this. If we do not have the experience of the incense, it is hard to offer the incense; we simply do not have it. We may have only the experience and enjoyment of Christ as the burnt offering and the meal offering. We may say that this is wonderful and adequate, but this is still in the outer court. We have to experience Christ more deeply. Then whenever we open our mouth, we will offer the incense instead of only the offerings. In this way, the function of the priests is always to minister Christ, not only to the people but also to God.

ALL OF GOD'S PEOPLE BEING PRIESTS

We should not say that the first priest in the Bible was Aaron or even Melchisedec. Abel made an offering to God (Gen. 4:4), and no doubt Adam already had done the same thing. Noah also offered to God as a priest (8:20), and Abraham, Isaac, and Jacob each built an altar and offered something to God (12:7; 26:25; 33:20). None of them when they offered sought an "official" priest to make the offering for them. This proves that every chosen person of God is a priest. As we have seen, a priest is one who serves God by enjoying God in Christ. God's intention is that all His people enjoy Him as priests. God's original intention was to present Himself as the tree of life to be enjoyed by man, and those who enjoy God the most are the priests.

In Egypt when all the people of Israel offered the Passover lamb, there was no official priest to do this for them. Rather, every family offered the Passover by themselves. This again shows that God intends all of His chosen ones to be the priests. After the people of Israel were brought out of Egypt and led to Mount Sinai, the Lord told them, "You shall be to Me a kingdom of priests and a holy nation" (Exo. 19:6a). It is as if He said, "I brought you out of Egypt to be a nation of priests. Every one of you is a priest. No one has any need to hire someone else. You yourselves are the priests."

ALL THOSE IN THE NEW JERUSALEM
BEING PRIESTS FOR ETERNITY

Revelation 20:6 speaks of those who will be priests for a thousand years, and 22:3 says, "His slaves will serve Him." To serve Him is to be a priest for eternity. Who will be the final priests? It will be all His redeemed ones, who share in the New Jerusalem. They will be the final priests eternally.

By all this we can see that our function as believers is not a small matter. We do not see much proper functioning among Christians today, because many do not have the adequate realization and experience. In these days, however, the Lord will recover our service. We will realize more and more, and we will come into more experiences of Christ. Then we will be able to function properly.

CHAPTER EIGHT

THE PRIESTHOOD

(2)

Scripture Reading: Gen. 1:26; Rev. 1:6; 20:6; 22:3-5

THE MINISTRY OF THE PRIESTS, THE KINGS, AND THE PROPHETS

In the entire Old Testament there are three kinds of offices, or ministries. In this respect, we can divide the thirty-nine books of the Old Testament into three groups. From Genesis to Ruth there is the ministry of the priests. In this portion of the Bible there are kings among the Gentiles, but there is no king among the people of God. Here we have only the priests. Then from 1 Samuel to Esther there are the kings. Then after Job through Song of Songs, from Isaiah to Malachi, there are the prophets. The priests, the kings, and the prophets are of three kinds of offices, or ministries.

It is after the degradation of the priesthood that the office of the kings was manifested. The last priest in this line was Samuel. Before him, the priests were Eli and his two sons. These two sons were an absolute failure in the priesthood, almost bringing an end to the priesthood at that time. Therefore, the Lord raised up little Samuel. Because Samuel was not a direct descendant of the family of Aaron, although he was of the tribe of Levi, we may say that the priesthood of Aaron at that time was ended by the two sons of Eli. The Lord raised up Samuel to be a priest to bring in the office of the king. This proves that the kingship was manifested due to the failure of the priesthood.

Later, the office of the prophets was raised up due to the

failure of the kings. Elijah and Elisha are the representatives of the prophets. They were raised up when the kingship, the ministry of the kings, became degraded, corrupted, and rotten. Even when King David failed by committing a sin, the prophet Nathan came in to function by speaking to the king (2 Sam. 12:1-12).

THE OFFICE OF THE PROPHET NEEDED
IN A SITUATION OF DEGRADATION

When the priesthood failed, the kingship came in, and when the kingship failed, the prophets came in. This indicates that the ministry of the prophets was not included in God's original intention. What God originally intended to have was the kingship and, even more, the priesthood. We were saved not mainly to be prophets but to be kings and priests. Revelation 1:5-6 says, "And from Jesus Christ, the faithful Witness, the Firstborn of the dead, and the Ruler of the kings of the earth. To Him who loves us and has released us from our sins by His blood and made us a kingdom, priests to His God and Father, to Him be the glory and the might forever and ever. Amen." This verse speaks of a kingdom and priests, but it does not mention prophets. This again indicates that we are saved to be kings and priests. Many Christians today want to have the gift of prophecy. There is not much teaching encouraging the believers to exercise the kingship and do the job of the priesthood. There is, however, too much teaching encouraging people to seek the gift of speaking.

According to 1 Corinthians 14, we can desire to be a prophet, but there is no need to desire to be a king or a priest. The kingship and the priesthood are ours by birth. We were reborn to be kings and priests. We may boldly declare, "Praise the Lord, I have been regenerated to be a king and a priest! I was born a king, and I was born a priest." First Peter 2:5 and 9 speak of the holy priesthood and the royal priesthood. We are kings as priests, so we have the kingly, royal priesthood. This is the same thought as in Revelation 1:6. On the other hand, 1 Corinthians 13:9 and 10 say concerning the gift of prophecy, "For we know in part, and we prophesy in part; but when that which is complete comes, that which is in part will be rendered useless." The office, the ministry, of the prophets will end at the coming of the Lord, but the kingship and priesthood will never end. We will be the priests and the kings forever and ever (Rev. 22:3, 5).

At the present time, however, we need the prophets when the priests are weak, the kings are rotten, and neither do their duty. Such a degraded situation compels the Lord to raise up the prophets. Today in Christianity many people appreciate the prophets, speakers, preachers, and ministers, but they have not enough regard for the priesthood and the kingship. This means that what the Lord desires to have is mostly neglected. Do we have the priesthood, the kingship, or simply the prophets? Too many today pay their attention only to the prophets, prophecy, speaking, and teaching. There is almost no kingship and priesthood.

Prophecy is a matter of a gift, but the priesthood and the kingship are matters of life. They are matters of our rebirth. We are all born to be priests and kings. If we prefer, we can desire the gift of prophecy, but this is not an item of our birthright. It is not solely a matter of life.

We must not pay too much attention to the gifts. The gifts were added in due to an abnormal condition. When the church is abnormal, we need a prophet, just as we need a doctor when our health is abnormal. We do not always have a doctor in our home, but we do always have a kitchen. Too often in a church there is the "dispensary" of the preachers, but there is no kitchen. We need food to be served more than we need medicine to be dispensed.

We were born to be kings and priests. If the church life is healthy and normal, there is not much need of the prophets. Instead, everyone functions as a priest. If everyone exercises the priesthood and the kingship, the prophets will have to find a job somewhere else. When the king fails, a "Nathan" comes, but if the priests with the kings are normal, there is no need for the prophets. First Corinthians 12 and 14 reflect an abnormal condition in the church in Corinth. Romans and Ephesians, however, reflect a normal condition. When we are in Ephesians and Romans, there is no need of 1 Corinthians 12 and 14, but when we are abnormal in the church life, we need the prophets; we need the gifts.

The church life is a life of the kings and the priests. It must not be a life of the prophets. If we need the prophets, we are degraded. We are in the "books of the prophets," which reveal a degraded condition. Since the generation of the apostles, it is because of degradation that the church has mainly had prophets and preachers. A great evangelist is the top preacher, the biggest speaker, but where are the priests and the kings? The Lord must recover the priesthood and the kingship.

Stanza 4 of *Hymns,* #848 says concerning the priesthood, "Through the church's degradation, / Saints this office desolate; / Through the weakness of their spirits / Preaching doth predominate." The priestly office is desolated through the church's degradation. In today's Christian churches we can hear much preaching, but when people are asked to pray, many are as silent as a tomb. When preaching predominates, it means that there is the ministry of the prophets, but there are no priests or kings. There is the gift, but there is no life. I say again, we were born to be priests and kings. The priesthood and the kingship are a matter of our new birth. If we want to have the gift of prophecy, we may desire it, but that is not something of our birthright.

As we have seen, the ministry of the prophets is needed because of the failure of the priests and kings. The prophets are needed to restore the priesthood and the kingship. Therefore, after the priesthood and the kingship are restored, there is no more need of the prophets. The office of the prophet was not in the original intention of God. In the original intention of God there were only two things: the priesthood and the kingship.

THE PRIESTHOOD AND THE KINGSHIP
BEING FOR GOD'S IMAGE AND DOMINION

There are two main aspects in the creation of man: image and authority, dominion (Gen. 1:26). Image refers to the expression of God, and dominion is for the representation of God to deal with His enemy. These two aspects were in God's original intention. From the very beginning God intended to have His expression and His representation. He created man with His image that man may be His expression, and He committed His authority to man that man may be His representative. From the beginning to the end of the Bible there are these two lines, the line of image and expression and the line of dominion and representation.

The priesthood is for the expression of God. The priests enjoy the Lord, and they become His expression, manifestation, habitation, and dwelling place. Through the priesthood God fully gains His image and expression. The kingship, on the other hand, is for authority and dominion. The kings represent God to deal with His enemy. These are the two items of the original intention of God.

We have seen that Revelation 1:6 speaks of the kingdom and priests. Verse 6 of chapter twenty also says, "Blessed and holy is he who has part in the first resurrection; over these the second death has no authority, but they will be priests of God and of Christ and will reign with Him for a thousand years." This verse speaks of priests and reigning kings but not of prophets. Of course, this verse is related to the millennium, the thousand years, but chapter twenty-two speaks of the situation in eternity. Verses 3 through 5 say, "And there will no longer be a curse. And the throne of God and of the Lamb will be in it, and His slaves will serve Him; and they will see His face, and His name will be on their foreheads. And night will be no more; and they have no need of the light of a lamp and of the light of the sun, for the Lord God will shine upon them; and they will reign forever and ever." The redeemed in eternity will serve the Lord before His face; this refers to the priesthood. Moreover, they will reign forever and ever; this is the kingship.

Please keep in mind that the priesthood is for expression, and the kingship is for representation. Both of these are matters of life, not of gift. Prophecy, however, is a matter of a gift, not of life. Even the Gentile prophet Balaam had the gift to prophesy, but he did not have the divine life.

THE KINGSHIP DEPENDING ON THE PRIESTHOOD

As we have said, the prophets were raised up entirely due

to the failure of the kings. The kingship, however, was raised up mostly due to the failure of the priesthood, but not entirely due to this failure. If the priesthood had not failed, there would still have been the need of the kingship. Zechariah 6:12 and 13 tell us that the Lord Jesus as the Builder of the temple is both the Priest and the King. God needs the kingship as well as the priesthood. However, we do not need prophecy if the priesthood and kingship are normal. We only need the prophets to recover the priesthood and the kingship when they are abnormal.

All the chosen people of God are intended to be priests and kings, but the kingship depends on the priesthood. This is why the Bible first speaks of the priesthood. This does not mean that we do not need the kingship, however. Rather, if the priesthood is strong, as it was at the time of Moses and Aaron, the kingship does not need to be manifested. It is when the priesthood weakens that the kingship is manifested. God's intention is not firstly the authority of the kingship. The first item of God's intention is to have His image. Eventually, though, we need both of these aspects.

The priesthood is the main item of God's intention, while the kingship is to match the priesthood. The first proper king was David. After David came to the throne, when he brought the Ark of Jehovah into his city, he girded himself with a linen ephod, which is the garment of the priests (2 Sam. 6:14). This indicates that although David was a king and the kingship at that time was strong, he realized that he still needed the priesthood. When in a church all the saints are strong in life, enjoying the Lord, feasting on Him, and functioning as priests, there is not much need for the kingship to be manifested. The purpose of the kingship is to rule, reign, maintain order, and deal with the enemy. When the children of God are strong in life and functioning as priests, everything is already in order. There is no special need for authority to maintain the order.

The eldership in the church is not a matter merely of the image of God but of the authority of God. In this sense, the elders are not mainly of the priesthood but of the kingship. We should not have too much eldership in the church. Rather, we must have the priesthood, and the more we have the priesthood, the better. However, when the priesthood becomes weak, we need the eldership, that is, the kingship. In the early days of the Brethren, for example, they had the priesthood without much need for authority. Later, however, when they lost the function of the priesthood, they emphasized the need for authority in the church.

We all are born again as priests. Therefore, we have to learn how to enjoy our birthright. We must learn how to live as priests enjoying Christ, contacting Him, feeding on Him, living by Him, putting Him on as our clothing, and taking Him as our dwelling place. When we enjoy Christ in such a way, we will have the priestly function of always ministering Christ both to God and to man. Then our church life will be very healthy and normal, and spontaneously out of this situation the authority of God will be realized. It is by the priesthood that we have the kingship.

In the proper church life, God is expressed and His authority is exercised. This is the priesthood plus the kingship. In such a situation, there is not much need for the office of the prophets. By the Lord's mercy we can testify that in some of our meetings for the Lord's table we have the priesthood with the kingship. There is no teaching, no exercise of the gifts, and no prophecy. There is simply the ministering of the priests with the kingship. When we come into such a meeting, we can sense the image, the expression, of God with His authority and representation; that is, we sense the priesthood and the kingship. That is the right and normal condition of the church. When we are weak, however, the priesthood is gone and the kingship disappears. Then the prophets rise up. To have the expression of Christ and the representation of God, and to not require prophecy, is the normal condition. This is what the Lord will recover. In the thousand year age and in eternity there will be no prophets. Even today in the Lord's recovery we can have a foretaste of the things to come.

TO HAVE AUTHORITY REQUIRING THE GROWTH OF LIFE

This is not a mere exhortation for us to function. We must realize that function is a matter of life. Therefore, we have to feast on the Lord, live by Him, and mingle with Him, as the priests did. This is why the first item we covered in the previous message was to see what a priest is. We must be that kind of person with that kind of life, enjoyment of life, and growth of life. Then we will be the right persons to express Christ. This is our function. Then along with this priesthood we will have the sense that the kingship also is here. The authority of God is exercised along with the image of God. Whenever we have the image of God, we have His authority. Adam was created in the image of God, so the authority of God was committed to him (Gen. 1:26). Authority always goes along with image.

It is by the priesthood with the kingship that the image of God is expressed and the authority of God is exercised. Revelation 20 and 22 tell us that both in the millennial kingdom and in eternity, when we will serve as priests, we will also reign as kings. Moreover, there will be no further need for the ministry of the prophets. I hope that by His mercy, the churches in all the localities may have a life full of the priesthood with the kingship, not requiring the ministry of the prophets; that is, that we would have much life without the need of much gift.

We may receive a gift without life, but we can never have authority in the church without life. If a brother is in the position of an elder but is short of the growth of life, gradually and eventually he will lose the real eldership, that is, the authority. However, the more a brother grows in life and is filled with the riches of Christ, even if he is not in the position of an elder, the brothers and sisters will realize that with him there is the authority. This is illustrated by the budding rod of Aaron in Numbers 17:2 through 8. The rod is a symbol of authority, and the budding of the rod is a matter of resurrection life. The authority among the Lord's children is a matter of life, not merely a matter of position. To elect a brother to be an elder does not work. We can place him in the position of an elder, but if he does not have the growth in life, his dead, lifeless "rod" will not bud. The kingship is a matter of life. Prophecy, on the other hand, is a matter of gift. We can receive the gift of prophecy quickly, but we cannot exercise the kingship in this way. The kingship depends on the growth of life. We have to feast on Christ, put on Christ, dwell in Christ, and be mingled with Christ. Christ must be wrought, woven, and mingled with us. Then we will have the measure of Christ to serve as priests. This is a matter of life, not of gift.

To one extent or another, we are all priests. Some may be bigger priests while some are smaller priests. Some may not be priests in the Holy of Holies, but by the Lord's mercy they are priests in the Holy Place. Others still may be priests in the outer court. Perhaps last year we were in the outer court, but this year we are in the Holy Place. Last year we may have known only how to offer the offerings, but this year we know how to offer the incense. Perhaps next year we will be priests in the Holy of Holies. For this we need the growth in life. The way to have the growth of life is by feeding and feasting on Christ.

THE PROPER PRIESTHOOD REQUIRING US TO KNOW AND DISCERN OUR SPIRIT

Hebrews 10:19 tells us to enter into the Holy of Holies. Only the priests can enter the Holy of Holies. In this way, the book of Hebrews confirms that we are the priests. If we were not priests, we would not be entitled to enter the Holy of Holies. Today the Holy of Holies is in our human spirit. Therefore, we need to learn how to know and discern the spirit (4:12; Rom. 8:6). Then we will know how to exercise our priesthood. If we do not know the spirit and cannot discern the spirit, it is hard to practice the priesthood. To know our human spirit is not mere doctrine. If we did not know where our mouth was, we could not eat. In the same way, we must be brought back to know our spirit, where we can contact the Lord.

I have the full assurance that the Lord will recover the enjoyment in our spirit for the proper priesthood and kingship. This is the Lord's recovery, which is a matter of His government. It is not a small matter to touch the government of the Lord. May the Lord be merciful to us that we would learn to know Him in a living way as the tree of life, to know the spirit, and to exercise the priesthood to enjoy Him. May the Lord be merciful that we would go to Him and stay with Him for some time about all these matters. We should pray over and pray regarding all these things. Then we will see that this is not merely a teaching. Rather, all these matters are for us to share in and enjoy.

ABOUT THE AUTHOR

Witness Lee was born in 1905 in northern China and raised in a Christian family. At age 19 he was fully captured for Christ and immediately consecrated himself to preach the gospel for the rest of his life. Early in his service, he met Watchman Nee, a renowned preacher, teacher, and writer. Witness Lee labored together with Watchman Nee under his direction. In 1934 Watchman Nee entrusted Witness Lee with the responsibility for his publication operation, called the Shanghai Gospel Bookroom.

Prior to the Communist takeover in 1949, Witness Lee was sent by Watchman Nee and his other co-workers to Taiwan to ensure that the things delivered to them by the Lord would not be lost. Watchman Nee instructed Witness Lee to continue the former's publishing operation abroad as the Taiwan Gospel Bookroom, which has been publicly recognized as the publisher of Watchman Nee's works outside China. Witness Lee's work in Taiwan manifested the Lord's abundant blessing. From a mere 350 believers, newly fled from the mainland, the churches in Taiwan grew to 20,000 in five years.

In 1962 Witness Lee felt led of the Lord to come to the United States, settling in California. During his 35 years of service in the U.S., he ministered in weekly meetings and weekend conferences, delivering several thousand spoken messages. Much of his speaking has since been published as over 400 titles. Many of these have been translated into over fourteen languages. He gave his last public conference in February 1997 at the age of 91.

He leaves behind a prolific presentation of the truth in the Bible. His major work, *Life-study of the Bible,* comprises over 25,000 pages of commentary on every book of the Bible from the perspective of the believers' enjoyment and experience of God's divine life in Christ through the Holy Spirit. Witness Lee was the chief editor of a new translation of the New Testament into Chinese called the Recovery Version and directed the translation of the same into English. The Recovery Version also appears in a number of other languages. He provided an extensive body of footnotes, outlines, and spiritual cross references. A radio broadcast of his messages can be heard on Christian radio stations in the United States. In 1965 Witness Lee founded Living Stream Ministry, a non-profit corporation, located in Anaheim, California, which officially presents his and Watchman Nee's ministry.

Witness Lee's ministry emphasizes the experience of Christ as life and the practical oneness of the believers as the Body of Christ. Stressing the importance of attending to both these matters, he led the churches under his care to grow in Christian life and function. He was unbending in his conviction that God's goal is not narrow sectarianism but the Body of Christ. In time, believers began to meet simply as the church in their localities in response to this conviction. In recent years a number of new churches have been raised up in Russia and in many eastern European countries.